Wittgenstein, politics and human rights

Books published under the joint imprint of LSE/Routledge are works of high academic merit approved by the Publications Committee of the London School of Economics and Political Science. These publications are drawn from the wide range of academic studies in the social sciences for which the LSE has an international reputation.

Wittgenstein, politics and human rights

Robin Holt

London and New York

First published 1997
by Routledge
11 New Fetter Lane, London EC4P 4EE

Simultaneously published in the USA and Canada
by Routledge
29 West 35th Street, New York, NY 10001

Typeset in Times by
BC Typesetting, Bristol

Printed and bound in Great Britain by
Mackays of Chatham PLC, Chatham, Kent

British Library Cataloguing in Publication Data
A catalogue record for this book is available from the British Library

Library of Congress Cataloging in Publication Data
Holt, Robin, 1966–
    Wittgenstein, politics and human rights/Robin Holt.
        p.   cm.
    Includes bibliographical references and index.
    1. Human rights.   2. Wittgenstein, Ludwig, 1889–1951
Contributions in political science.   I. Title.
JC571.H615   1997
323′.01–dc21   96-39528
                                         CIP

ISBN 0–415–15438–3

Contents

Acknowledgements

My deepest thanks go to John Lee for starting it all off, to Brian Barry and Stephen Mulhall for guidance during the period when this text was but a thesis, and to my colleagues at Southampton, especially Dennis McManus, Ray Monk, Liam O'Sullivan, and David Owen. Nice One. I would also like to thank Maria Stasiak for copy-editing and all at Routledge for their continued help and direction.

Abbreviations

References to Wittgenstein's works are from the following:

BB   *The Blue and Brown Books*, Blackwell (2nd edn), 1972.
C&V   *Culture and Value*, ed. G.H. von Wright, trans. P. Winch, Blackwell, 1989.
LA   *Lectures and Conversations on Aesthetics, Psychology and Religious Belief*, ed. C. Barret, Blackwell, 1970.
NB   *Notebooks 1914–1916*, trans. G.E.M. Anscombe, Blackwell, 1969.
OC   *On Certainty*, ed. G.E.M. Anscombe, G.H. von Wright, trans. D. Paul and G.E.M. Anscombe, Blackwell, 1969.
PI   *Philosophical Investigations*, trans. G.E.M. Anscombe, Blackwell, 1963
PR   *Philosophical Remarks*, trans. R. Hargreaves and R. White, Blackwell, 1990.
RC   *Remarks on Colour*, ed. G.E.M. Anscombe, trans. L. McAlister and M. Schättle, Blackwell, 1990.
RFM   *Remarks on the Foundations of Mathematics*, ed. G.H. von Wright, R. Rhees and G.E.M. Anscombe, trans. G.E.M. Anscombe, Cambridge University Press, (revised edn), 1983.
T   *Tractatus Logico Philosophicus*, trans. D.F. Pears and B.F. McGuinness, Routledge, 1989.
WL   *Wittgenstein's Lectures, Cambridge 1932–1935*, ed. A. Ambrose, Rowman and Littlefield, 1979.
Z   *Zettel*, ed. G.E.M. Anscombe and G.H. von Wright, trans. G.E.M. Anscombe, Blackwell, 1967.

Introduction
Why Wittgenstein?

You can't *build* clouds. And that's why the future you *dream* of
never comes true.

(C&V, p. 41)

CONTRACTING AND HUMAN RIGHTS

As the frontiers of cultures, nations, traditions, habits and natural
conditions which once were alien, inhospitable, inexplicable, difficult
and mysterious are increasingly contained and purged of their otherness it appears that a practice of universally applicable and ethically
primary rules governing all human relations is at least an imaginable
endeavour. But what rules can afford us such a perspective? At the
risk of sounding overtly Social Darwinist the most blatant are those
linked to material exchange. Despite the presence of recalcitrant
pockets of mediævalist cultural warriors fundamentally opposed to
the ebb and flow of global principles, rooted as they see them in the
lusty posturing of spiritually bankrupt egos, the large majority of
us are embroiled in activities of production and exchange. We are,
it seems, as developed versions of the Enlightenment's *homo oeconomicus*, forever chasing the shrink-wrapped bandwagon; subjected by
and subjectifying of the rules of the market. This structural syntax
of material efficiency, effectiveness and circulation requires an 'us'
which is individualist and dualist. The human being has a separate
identity, divided between work and leisure, one fuelling the other.
The hues of this identity, the variety of being, is of surface relevance
alone; beneath our outward distinctions there is a common core identity, an individual, concerned to earn access to spaces from which
they can articulate themselves, concerned, that is, to engage in
exchange and production to articulate and enhance their lives.

The loci of twenty-four-hour global media, trans-national corporations, international treaties, conventions and agreements on trade and resource containment, science, wars and even sport are transforming what was once a medley of rich and often conflicting cultures into a single, thematic interchange of practices whereby common understanding becomes little more than the communication of pragmatic intent given the confines of the effective means to economic trade and the production and exchange of information. This commercialization links us all, and in this respect the impact of our actions comes to have global implications.[1] Production and exchange is now near universal in its purposes and techniques, its electronic tropes connect the most diverse of people and places. It provides a vast repository of metallic knowledge embodied by practices of value measurement which in some way or other resonate throughout the human condition – one we can assess, compare, reduce, construct or divide. Conceived by the Enlightenment *Philosophes* as resources rationally to be assessed and controlled our environments have increasingly succumbed to measurement in terms of relative scarcity. Devoid of any intrinsic meaning they are parcelled up and distributed according to the relative, competitive display of autonomous claimants. Trade has quantified the world by casting humanity in the mould of homogenous choosers with the potential reasonably to discuss and agree to guides for the good life, understood in economic terms,[2] free from the voodoo of localized immersion. Less a disenchantment of the world than a shift from the spiritual to the commercial, white goods have replaced the White Goddess as that which commands veneration.

But this condition is far from stable, indeed it thrives on motion, and thus we are tempted, when undergoing the common rush for the often very real material benefits made possible by the practice of economic enterprise, to grope for handrails of generality, lines of certitude, to steady and re-direct ourselves when we stumble, are pushed, blocked, trampled or sent the wrong way. We are prone to invoke principles which act like some river bedrock, channelling the heady flow with its eddies, currents and pools of calm, which ensure that our activity does not spill over into some indeterminate, directionless mess. Being a being for whom efficiency and effectiveness are becoming increasingly important, *homo oeconomicus* uses principles erring on the side of rational procedure – debated, agreed, codified, and consistently, openly and coherently applied. This suggests that we value such principles for their utility as structures of control; but when looked at in *use* this value is suggestive not only of a calculated means–end reasoning, but an expression of a subjective, even intrinsic sanctity of life. It is to the exploration of the most emblazoned of these principles that this book is devoted: human rights.

Initially invoked as a declaration against the 'final solutions' bred in the paranoia of fascistic anti-politics human rights have emerged as claims it is legitimate to invoke in response to a myriad of problems encountered by people as contractors in their contractual relations.[3] They have become claims to be defined in terms of possessive title – we invoke rights as things which are owned and used like amulets to ward off uncertainty. From Locke onwards[4] property configurations determined by self-governing title holders have formed a primary object for theoretical conceptions of justice in the West. The most recent variation on this theme of justice as a price system comes from modern contractarian justice theorists. Their stories tend to involve an abstracted group of people gathered together in a hypothetical scenario of isolation and innocence contrived through informational 'veils'. Resembling some form of crude bazaar the characters, upon encountering each other, have to take general decisions as to which principles for governing their subsequent (presumably communal) lives they would all bargain towards were their own conceptions of what was good to be best realized. In these fictitious political Edens it is usually some type of human rights system which articulates the point at which their considerations reach unity; one which goes on to inform any resultant institutional practices which may be subsequently decided upon. Without the observance of these primary rights there would be no sense to the idea of a meaningful bargain, no possibility of a political society of *agents*, and no continuity or coherence to concepts of authority, obligation, punishment, consent and rule.

Human rights as limiting aspects of prevailing practices of production and exchange have adopted the norms of this exchange behaviour; we buy and sell what we see as good and bad by establishing contracts, with ground rules, and in doing so empower ourselves by virtue of our being able to realize our interests and identity with the minimum sacrifice of self-control and self-articulation. What is of interest for us equates with what, under specific mediums of possession and control, acquires interest. Worth is what we decide it is, embodied by the free interchange of information and goods in bargaining-led structures. Human rights act as defenders of the space that enables these decisions to be taken and articulated. As inviolable claims to personal room they allow us to resist the cultural imposition of rules and practices which we feel deny the value inherent in our being able to stand back from our surrounding regimes and ask just what it is we want to *become*, whilst still allowing us access to those very same regimes which enable such questions to move beyond the mere expression of solipsistic anguish. We invoke human rights in ways akin to the use of commodities, signs, logos and currency; they symbolize the inherent value of what *lies behind*. The logic of human rights rests on the assumption that questions of being and identity are inextricably linked with questions of doing, more specifically, the becoming of a value-laden subjective self in a quantifiable world of fact using the language of rational and quantifiable choice sets which can be measured and compared through a reductionist analysis which treats all relations as transactions accountable in themselves;[5] it gives meaning to the question of what is and is not of value, viz., that which reasonable and rational choice expresses irrespective of the content of such choice. Value is an aspect of the ontological premise that we can possess the world as something which brings us marginal utility.

The characteristics of these human rights most usually include the following: *universality,* they act in the interests of everyone at all times; *primacy,* they 'trump' all other decisional considerations; *fundamental ethical status,* they are deserving of unqualified respect because of the equal 'worth' of the human soul or identity and its interests and life plans; they are *manifest,* they exist independently of whether they are put into effect in any one context; they are *individualist,* they take the interests of the individual person above consequential considerations; and *species specificity,* they apply to all and only humans as 'a common standard of achievement for all peoples and all nations'.[6] This common standard is not elliptical or ephemeral in its nature, but overt. Human rights, it seems, enable us not only to focus our needs, but to do so explicitly through measurement. To avoid being swallowed by techno-babble and trends of materialization we invoke limits which articulate the fear of enclosure and the desire to manipulate consequent upon focusing on being through the lens of material living. In this way the right to life becomes the extent to which good health care, basic subsistence and laws of redress are provided (how much is spent on them) rather than an intangible sense of well-being. The right to be free from torture equates with the number of unjustified and unexplained arrests coupled with the testaments of survivors, and not with more endemic systems of general though unarticulated psychological and physiological suffocation. The right to subsistence equates with the right to a job and holidays with pay rather than the often convoluted or disturbingly passionate articulation of indigenous, self-sufficient bonds of immediacy. The rights to free association, speech and equal participation rest on the open provision of equal opportunities into established social systems such voting or lobbying, rather than the creation, destruction and re-creation of grammatical systems of identity.

We have a tendency to see rights in terms of lists which give fixed meaning to the idea of injustice, meanings which are universal to the extent that they are used by people in universal, generalized con-ditions – the dominant one, hypothetically conceived as contract, being the trade in goods and information. Though fixed in terms of their focusing upon the primacy of subjective worth, human rights adapt in line with the material capacity of provision and the dis-solving of difference. Historically an insurance policy taken out by the American Founding Fathers and the citizens of the French Revo-lution to assure the integrity and validity of subjects suffused in nat-ural law, the policy renewals of subsequent generations have increasingly focused upon requirements for protection against the ravages of need, to the extent that human rights now encompass first-order claims to non-interference in life, liberty and estate made subject to second-order material claims for subsistence and well-being. Added to this has recently been the call for a third order of collective rights which acknowledge the importance of cultural and ethnic practices *to the autonomous subject* along with a growing awareness of the specification[7] of persons enjoying rights manifest in concerns over gender, mental and physical capacities, maturity and even more speculatively future generations, certain animals and the environment at large. Metaphysical phantasmagorias they may have been when invoked as abstracted crystallizations of some stoical *pneuma*, but their use is now of a more prosaic and pressing nature in which specific equalities and grievances are addressed in specific contexts. They encompass very real demands made upon the body politic by those who feel alienated, dispossessed and disquieted by the power machinations of found regimes of exchange. Arendt's insight on the erosion of substantive and unquestioned value systems is instructive here, because human rights discourse has expanded in line with a collapse in faith amongst the collective consciousness.[8] They inaugurate a revolutionary shift in perspective from a filial loyalty to virtue to self-reliant will; from self-consciously immersed proponents of value systems to self-reliant consciousnesses. Exponents of virtue are subsumed by procedural officers – people for whom justice and politics involve the instantation of voluntarily established systems of value-neutral rule.

The expansion of human rights discourse to cover specific instances of bias, oppression and grievance in line with the felt experience of isolate individuals has, however, a tendency to belittle their use. As is the problem with many lists, including those of claims, they tend to grow, to the extent as Kundera recognizes, that the world and everything in it risks becoming a right;[9] and so the widening breadth of conceptualizations of the concept expands it into meaninglessness. The argument over human rights becomes a kind of limbo contest – how low can they go without collapsing into clichéd generalities? Keeping them tied to practice of exchange seems to provide an identifiable threshold – human rights can be extended to those whose familiarity with conceptual bargaining positions is demonstrative of a capacity for reason and rationality. This can be extended to groups and the like only as facilitating conditioners or potential objects of reflection and not as prime agents. This suggests human rights are indubitably bound up with beings for whom moral progress is a discernible and possible if not probable historical motion and hence are specific to instances of potential, self-directed will. Without this deontic norm, which is not a proof of realism but an assertion of rational consistency and coherency, they lose definition and force.

If the thematic element of value in exchange and the limits to exchange is emphasized as *the* common denominator to modern human activity then the claim to possess human rights becomes a cry for the creation and protection of gaps defined by their material absence within which an agent is free to act. This space is not something quantifiable as such, but is manifest in the capacity to follow practices of commodification without becoming commodified; to sell without being sold. In commodified guise the world becomes increasingly uninterested in distinction. There is neither perspective nor a sense of process in the commercial world view. Interfering with the sanctity of market-orientated space is taboo, as is interference with the sanctity of core identities. Postulating limits on interference allows us to equalize and regulate our condition without *conditioned* recourse to the scalar practices which stratify such conditions. We are isolating the ghost in the machine – a seat of universal perspective which requires little more than the co-ordination and management of universal bargaining conditions. The evil other is interference itself, that which seeks to dictate the parameters and conditions of full productive bargaining with a view to control by virtue of information deprivation, opaque machinations, overt dogma and unruly disruption.

Human rights inhabit the edges between inviolable spheres of mind and market allowing the former to desist from force and the latter to resist mystificatary interference from would-be social engineers. They list formal conditions of unconditionality that enable us to be free from discrimination and oppression whilst following our *personal* life plans, provided that in doing so we avoid the public instituting of those plans to an extent that interferes with the equal rights of others still to effectively engage with life on their own terms, from their own perspective. The frenetic, immediate and opaque character-istics of material exchange do little to foster security, and human rights help anchor activity in an alternative source of comfort – a doubting and hence certain subjective core. There is a symbiotic rela-tionship between human rights and the objects of their wrath – to work effectively and efficiently markets require limits to their ram-pant and often random expansion; these are set by the private worlds of individual will. To become sensible individual wills require arenas of free expression, regimes of articulation, and these are pro-vided by minimal but universal rules of exchange and contract which ensure that the *interests*[10] of subjects are fully articulated.

Paradoxically this urge to sustain our individuality rests upon a philosophical claim to sameness rooted in the neo-Kantian desire to see the presence of natural and social phenomena as morally irre-levant; being moral is an attribute all rational beings necessarily possess to the same degree by virtue of their prospective freely cast will. Irrespective of specific instances of time and place we are able to suppose a noumenal thread enabling subjective experiences of time and place to persist. We can identify, though never phenomen-ally know, a fundamental point of access to the world, a moment where control and responsibility is the subject's alone. What is required is the courage to use *our own understanding* of ourselves as freely intelligible beings capable of transcending cultural and empir-ical confinement. The usual justification of human rights has it that irrespective of the nature of actions themselves there is an essential, non-reducible self-governing core to the agent, the transcendental subjectifying subject, which as the seat of all potential configurations of what is good, beautiful and true is worthy of respect from all other agents: that condition of universality which is willed for its own sake as the condition of freedom. Love thy neighbour as thou would thyself because in essence we are of the same stuff. In pre-serving this sameness we can confront and confirm the confusion and complexity of commodified living whilst resisting the socialistic or romantic urge to fuse being with heteronomous activity. The connexion between our social condition and individual will is one where it is our duty to submit the former to constant subjection by the latter[11] in order for its continued definitive (as a norm) survival, and human rights are the claims enabling us to do this.

This position exemplified by human rights is not one of crude equality based on exact resemblance but an acknowledgement that to the extent people are ends in themselves, they have unique life plans conceived from what is without and articulated through regimes, they are equal as potential founders of identity and there exist no rational grounds for differential treatment. No one self can be treated as prior to another *in this respect*[12]. This reciprocity is the driving force for the principles of equal consideration of interest and non-interference,[13] principles which ought to permeate all enactments of control amongst the motion of the regime; either of subject on subject or of the subjection on others. To claim human rights is to acknowledge what is essential and definite to our selves as plan-makers:[14] a kind of bell jar defined by the limits of the regime.[15] We have no absolute knowledge of this arena, save for an imaginative appreciation of the consequences of its non-being – namely the dissolution of stability, equilibrium, persistence, progression, responsibility, prediction and the like. This synthetic *a priori* status lends human rights the badge of Kantian category – that which must be pre-supposed lest we collapse into structural puppets; flotsam and jetsam on the regimented tides of control.

So the stuff of life is being confined to an inner core; the only area, it is supposed, where we can challenge the untidiness of manifest difference with the singular perfection of that bloodless entity – the mind. By collapsing the world into a dichotomy Kant's practical reasoner is a real-time version of the Cartesian *cogito*[16] whereby the 'I' has determination and temporality – a being whose doubt confines the subtlety, complexity and diversity of everyday experience to the status of obstacles in understanding: a kind of white noise interrupting the transmission of metaphysical profundity. The *cogito*, suspicious of inevitably confusing, unreliable, doubtful and valueless substance retreats to the 'mirrored certainty' of its own thought; the *cogito* as the always renewed event of thought. I cannot doubt that I think and to think I must be. To doubt I must first be. Doubt, thought and being (all of which are known by all by virtue of their doubting, thinking and being and hence require no pre-existing truth or knowledge) coincide to frame an entirely privileged first cause from which other objectivities can be drawn (e.g. one of my ideas is that of infinity, hence there must be a God) but none of which pre-exist the *cogito*. Meaning, knowledge and understanding become mental certainties transferred from the inner to the outer by means of language, communication. They remain, then, uniquely attached to a doubting, thinking, being.

This dualism forms the precursor of much current human rights reasoning which continues to conceive the identity of subjects as an authentic, pre-determined and persistent unity capable of linking past, present and future actions in a nexus of conscious understanding, intention, choice and responsibility. Politics becomes the institutional articulation of subjective integrity – a necessary restraining activity for the protection and promotion of mental fabrications called separate interests, an activity which whilst it ideally and enthusiastically (enthusiasm being for Kant the 'passionate involvement in good'[17]) seeks its own annihilation in utopian regimes of perfect autonomy acknowledges that this liberty, which must come from within the individual as internal law-giver, is not perfectly felt and so requires reminders in the form of laws and principles constructed hypothetically in the guise of a social contract; the progenitor of the ideal liberal regime. The Cartesian and Kantian emphasis upon the subject resulted in a politics which eschewed the paranoid desire for good or peaceful and stable government orientated around the Princely concepts of charisma, ruthlessness and sagacity established in relation to the passive mob held morally inert by ignorance, original sin and cupidity, and politically stable by hierarchical duty-bound regimes of control. Individualistic exchange relations permeated the sanctum of the Caliph appropriating for the agent the sovereign perspective as they went. This is less a radical inversion of the relationship between ruler and ruled[18] than the subsuming of responsibility for rule by the ruled. Human rights articulate the claim for autonomy, for self-rule, and the resultant political subjects end up like the bottles on an apothecary's shelf; contained in neat and regimented equilibrium, none polluting the other and each fully identified and labelled as being free, capable and of intrinsic worth.

In delineating private from public spheres on universal moral grounds human rights sustain both the subject and the regimes sustaining the idea of the subject – providing one with the rejuvenating, creative inputs necessary for adaptation and the other with the protection from impersonal power and control necessary to cultivate personal fulfilment. The persisting regimes embodying current social living are often complex, bureaucratic, huge and impersonal – their bewildering array of access and drop-out points provide the ideal flux within which a universally valid moral core *in the individual* gains credence as a source of bedrock and certainty. The ideal is no longer who we are but the creation of de-ontological space enabling us to conceive and resist what we definitely are not or do not want to be.[19]

BARRIERS TO BARGAINING

Communitarian perspectives seek to erode these distinctions established by the liberal addiction to the inviolability of inner, personal space by questioning the intelligibility of a core identity. The liberal or contractarian conception of human rights as protecting and promoting the exercise of autonomy, defined variously as a combination of free choice, voluntary obligation and individual responsibility,[20] lies, it is supposed, naked, isolate and devoid of situation. As subjects we are subjectified not by doubt or reason but the variety of social practices of which we are a constituent part. Subjects cannot be viewed, even hypothetically, as isolate choosers in an unbiased, measured framework (moral bargainers) because what makes us who we are as humans are the very characteristics human rights reasoning conceives as morally irrelevant. Focusing on the ghost leaves us nothing of substance – a variant of the fact–value problematic in which there is no explanation of how we shift from spirit to person. A host of unencumbered, mutually indifferent entities inhabiting communities which are nothing more than procedural amalgams of rational choice sets is just a homogenous ideal. Humans are human because of the rules, habits, traditions, rituals, relations and narratives which enable us to take a stand and to choose in the first place. This is a resurrection of participation politics – no longer is the public merely a medium of exchange, but a multiplicity of regimes populated by the suspicious, the fervent, the committed, the idiosyncratic, the flaccid, the reasonable, the lost and found, the expectant and the forlorn all of whom are characterized as they are not by virtue of a self-directing will[21] but by revelation, experience, birth and other social bonds. The world comes to have a jelly bean, multi-flavoured quality which at times becomes slightly sickly; excessive revelling in one's heritage is not so far from inculcating the nonage which human rights reasoning so urgently sought to redress.

But the point of community as conditional of and necessary to the idea of subject and identity is a crucial one for from this embedded perspective human rights are the birth-child of a specific tradition. They have emerged from a specific narrative crucible as a response to specific problems cast in a specific world view which remains distinct from and not necessarily relevant to other traditions. The implications for universal principles like human rights are apparently devastating. Whilst it is still a legitimate ethical claim to say that *from within* the liberal perspective human rights are better seen as expressions of the creative and expressive use of language by agents hewn from the Western, democratic rock as it were, it need not be the case that such a rendering of rights makes them any more attractive as ethical precepts to those people who actively resist the apparent individualism inherent in rights use. Environmentalists, transcendentalists, anarchists, conservatives and fundamentalists can all in some way or other renounce the force of human rights as presently conceived within the confines of the liberal democratic hegemony on grounds such as: nature having intrinsic value; the autonomous soul being a barrier to be transcended on the eightfold path to Nirvana; autonomy under governments being a sham; freedom being a secondary aspect to constitutional tradition or a necessarily complete abeyance to divine interdicts. Even within the tradition human rights claims can remain essentially contested, being understood as an acknowledgement of natural law, pragmatically, morally or legally. We can dispense with human rights as metaphysical companions to the self as it journeys toward the rational godhead; indeed we need not look at them in eschatological or diachronic terms at all, seeing them purely as a way of expressing ethical concerns currently in vogue amongst specific types.

Human rights are not as starkly individualist as all this communitarian posturing suggests. The Universal Declaration, for example, states that people 'are endowed with reason and conscience and should act towards one another in a spirit of brotherhood' (art. 1); that the family is 'the natural and fundamental unit of society' (art. 16) and that 'Everyone has duties to the community in which alone the free and full development of his personality is possible' (art. 29). The International Covenant on Civil and Political Rights establishes the right to self-determination of peoples (art. 1) and 'the right, in community with other members of their group, to enjoy their own culture, to profess and practice their own religion, or to use their own language'.[22] It is clear that rights are used by virtue of their being expressive of established practices valued as mediums of expression for the subject, and if the communitarian critique consisted solely in swiping at a supposed indifference to context then it would be worthy of little attention. Human rights are concepts founded on and adapted to conditions of bargaining, exchange and interest articulation and have sense to the extent that they facilitate such processes. The more global the economy, the more the felt need for autonomous interest articulation. But the critique is dependent upon engaging beyond this surface conflict, because on its view not only are human rights neither universal nor primary in appeal but only in aspiration, they are actually damaging if seen as such because of their false ontology. In not recognizing the ontological necessity of being embedded in established social narratives of which there are inevitably many, human rights can actually fragment identity, encouraging us to create an artificial amalgam of homogenized, dispossessed individuals which we hold as an ideal; as opposed to enabling us to recognize a constellation of deliberative cultures within which people invoke qualitatively different readings of the good life to inform their decisions and actions. The resultant liberal types are of a distasteful appearance – assertive, insular, aggressive, managerial and the like. They are beset with neuroses of control, of independent form and of prediction. Without a swift recapitulation of its atomized doctrines the liberal world, which means most of the world, will collapse into selfish 'warre'.

To the extent human rights ignore this attachment they presuppose a world in which we are all ultimately the same, and this imposes a rational, egotistical abstraction upon the very real qualitative differences between us, one which risks creating a distopian, atomized uniformity that seeks to erode the prodigious diversion of traditions of which we are a part. The human condition is not, as may be supposed, ultimately about isolate choosers, but peoples manifest as archipelagos of constitutive activity such as religion, gatherings of friends, clubs, hobbies, political parties, interest groups and numerous other instances of collective enterprise. We must recognize that we develop a conception of the self at this partial, communal level, and to the extent that human rights veil this understanding they should be challenged as pedalling a misbegotten ontology. Politics becomes the negotiation of temporary equilibrium between embedded difference whereby a *modus vivendi* between historical communities is wrought out of a recognition of mutually embodied subjects. There is little point in bargaining over universal principles such as rights – rather we must just reveal and revel in our embedded situations; the subject is self-effacing, suffused in localized ideas of the good which frame their world views beyond which lies the realm of the infidel and the metic. As such it is overtly negative – to aspire to the beyond is to betray the past, present and future of the now – politics is the assertion of communal and not subjective integrity. To put it crudely the debate seems pre-disposed to form two fairly rigid camps – either we are embedded selves and rights are cultural products with a specific narrative heritage and necessarily limited appeal, or we are *noumena* and they are universal expressions of freely willed reason. One camp sees freedom and originality of identity lying in the shedding of social garb, the other has it lying in the very donning of that garb.

CONFESSION, NOT BARGAINING

To reduce linguistic relations to logical, contractual forms or to communal edicts; to confine sense to atomized or communal knowledge and information; and to define power in the limits of individual sovereignty or cultural taboo as do both liberals and communitarians belies the tragedy, fecundity, absurdity and comedy of human action – what Austin termed the inevitable suffering of pretence and excuse. It is when set against the intractable poles of the political 'debate'[23] between the universalist/individualist strains and the communitarian/group strains that Wittgenstein's philosophical programme to resist continually the urge to speak from beyond the ordinary, to challenge any conceptions of the absolute not with alternatives but on grounds of intelligibility, offers not a way forward in the sense of providing the correct synthesis, but a clarification of just what the attempt to define concepts like human rights, identity and the human self involves. He shows how as language users humans are embedded in grammar (the criteria by which we come to experience understanding, knowledge, wisdom and a sense of place) that is both bewitching and enabling. Bewitching because its limits, what we cannot say, seem to point to there being something outside of what we cannot say, when what is not remains ineffable. Enabling because it is the very impossibility of being unable to step outside ordinary language that ensures no cultural force nor universal principle is immune from the fragmentation of circumstance, invention and chance within which our responsibilities are wrapped.

That we talk of ourselves as separate souls, or as cultural products, means we tend to think that we must indeed be of such stuff, and this either–or conceptualizing of the problem creates identity illusion. Identity for Wittgenstein does not stem from the isolation of causal parts, but from the contexts of grammatical expression which themselves have no invariant or solid limits, but fluid or probable ones. The use of language, the ways in which we engage with each other, involves encounters with these fluid boundaries; we rub up against and struggle with the limits of meaning, with differences, with other-ness. Conceptual confusion comes in attempting to go beyond these boundaries in order to propose alternatives which are somehow closer to the truth, which present the individual with even greater closure of meaning, which try to tell the individual where to go, how to move and what to believe. It is this whole process of driving piles into the swamp in order to further secure for ourselves an ontological bedrock in either an inviolable self or else in one's cultural orbits that is nonsensical, if it is assumed that the resultant intellectual motion represents an eschatological shift from one given to another of greater perspicuity. By looking at language, as opposed to the self or cultural groups, the whole idea of predictable givens like human rights comes into question; language, as Wittgenstein investigates it, is never absolutely fixed in its restraints but, potentially, open and diverse.

The ambience of Wittgenstein's work lies not in its espousal of certain, ideological truths, but in its awareness of distinction. To use Foucault's terminology, using language is like herding the chaotic, the discontinuous and the abrupt with tools of exclusion (taboo, rejection and so on), commentary (reproduction and emasculation) and technique (education, controlled signs),[24] but only for it to break free again further up or down or to the side of the trail and so roam, awaiting further capture in some other context. It is in language that we control, and in language we resist. Language is not something we can dominate, or escape, but use. Such use is not mere imitation, but the acknowledgement of certain rules which are *appropriated and re-appropriated* in different contexts such that the initial aim of the rule is replaced by another given its re-deployment in a different context by different peoples. To use language is to create; it is, as de Certeau says, to construct from established rules, to establish relations with interlocutors and to carve out a present relative to our contextual time and place.[25]

As moments of grammatical capture in the regime of market rela-tions human rights have been very successful in confining and salving angst. By providing spaces of legitimated resistance they provide for a channelling of grief and concern which flow into and are dealt with by institutional procedures, sensitive to the strength and direc-tion of such flows. But this legitimization of resistance does not exhaust its possibility as both the liberals, who are generally well pre-disposed to it, and the communitarians, who generally conceive it as fragmentary, atomist and insensitive, seem to believe. The former see problems as ones of application, the latter as ones of conception, and for both the remedy lies in replacement, either of the minutiae or of the informing ideal. The grammatical perspective on such rights lends a much more complex view of their use, for the very capture of meaning in the institutional space of the regime requires an identification and exploration of possible lines of escape. Being imbued with rules of the regime requires modes of use which bend, meld and fragment the spaces depending upon the conditions of their occupation. Human rights have shifted in focus and force not because of any greater knowledge of their subject matter, the human self, nor because of any greater revelatory sense of right and wrong, but as a result of grammatical motion – the ignorance, cunning, misery, joy, sagacity and myriad of other states which inform appropriations of such rules.

Human rights discourse has had a tendency to cover this frission behind the 'specious splendour' of their institutionalized being, as witnessed by innumerable international treaties to which all and sundry, from social democracies to demagogues, clamour to sign up. That the proliferation of human rights in terms of their scope, their specificity and their universalist integrity has done little to alleviate instances of cruelty which almost seem an endemic aspect of the human condition is an observation given testament to by nightly media broadcasts and the experience of millions. Attractive and inspirational when encoded, in speech *act* their legacy is less than encouraging. In response to this failure to ameliorate suffering the tendency has been to attempt corrections of modes of application; to fine-tune and extend legal codes and executive means of enforcement, or alternatively to replace rights as badges of autonomy with rights as badges of group integrity, with little or no reflection on the shifting narrative roles such rights can or do play within regimes of production and exchange. The concept of legitimate resistance is conceived as the working for better enforcement of a necessary and known ideal, and human rights are used to provide the stratified individualist spaces within which such projects can be considered. By confining the idea of resistance to continued moments of further capture manifest in the effective and efficient spread of atomized relations exemplified by human rights discourse the sustenance of the regimes of production and exchange is seen to be further ensured; fed by the continued control of resistance. In resisting the system in terms of its praxis participants are proselytizing the theory; as embodied by the ideal code of human rights. A theory which is exclusionary in its appeal to an originating subject, the rejection of which is considered manifest insanity, in its invocation of a codicly assumed authority deemed applicable in all political arenas, and in its requirement of an educative stage setting of a predominantly contract-orientated, liberal-democratic hue.

Despite *and because* of this sense of architectural presence human rights discourse is able to yield an array of meaningful descriptions. They could be a cry for help from felt oppression, an acknowledgement of universal reason, a scheme of international recognition, an indicator of an assertive, male mentality, an ethnocentric, totemistic group expression, or, much like Sailor's snakeskin jacket in the film *Wild at Heart*, a symbol of individuality and personal freedom – a practical, a moral, a political, a gender, a cultural or a symbolic description. Each has sense from within a regime of production and exchange, a sense which further secures their use and hence enhances in some respect the continued workings of the regime. But imaginative, non-legitimate resistance which seeks, in exploring the limits of human rights discourse, to challenge the reasons why those limits are established is also possible, and far from being mere instances of ignorance and insanity, taking a linguistic perspective as is urged by Wittgenstein allows us to envisage these as potentially meaningful responses to the regime itself; responses predicated not on more refined modes of implementation of an ideal but an erosion of the ideal as an intelligible claim; responses not in terms of goals but conditions, including those of the self. To be a linguistic self is to be in proximity with, to imbibe and to articulate disciplinary mechanisms, codes and established relations of the regime, it is to accept that there is no escape from framing conditions, but to see that such conditions are not necessarily hegemonic, to be resented, to be met with resistance from alternative hegemonies in some form of eternal battle; to see that such conditions when appropriated shift in novel narrative use.

Thus the same goes for the communitarian critique of ontic conditions of individualism; whilst it may make no sense to regard the subject as primary to context, nor does it make sense to merely reverse the logic and see context as primary. Both individualists and communitarians risk partaking of *the* ideal; they sing to a single tune and display a concern for establishing the correct rhythm and tempo – whilst there may actually be no one correct way. To follow the rules of music is to interpret, to acknowledge the intentions of the composer, the expectations of the audience, the competency of the musicians, the purpose of the occasion, and in such action the idea of there being a single mode of competence seems puzzling; what matters are the nuances, the trivialities, the complexities of the narrative moments which provide the rule follower with moments of potential change.[26] Being captured by cultural rules does not imply we are cultural products, but linguistic beings.

So human rights can form a frame of articulation, but this is not the only way in which they can be sensibly used, for resistance need not take the form of knowledge. Though at times solid enough – we see about us an age of science, technology and material trade – we cannot *know* whether this is an age set for oblivion or whether, in Wittgenstein's words, it is destined to become one of the most enduring things in the modern world – a stable unit of perspective.[27] The future is unknowable, but not unimaginable, the architecture of regimes is always subject to erosion, directions and even co-ordinates change, and that human rights have seemingly found resonance in moving in one way in conjunction with this technological world is no reason or justification for their being somehow right or wrong *per se*. We often seek to explain and legitimate experiences through classification and identity, a practice which generalizes the idea of isolate subject or contextual vessel to explain the singularity or the commonality of utterances. Wittgenstein saw this generalism as an unhealthy, distasteful habit of thought. But equally he was pessimistic as to the possibilities of any remedy,[28] indeed remedies themselves are often not answers, but further confusions which replace one generality or mode of classification with another; in the instance of individualism versus communitarianism, the replacement of absolute autonomy with tepid contingency.

Philosophy for Wittgenstein is not in the business of providing remedies, blueprints, ideals, answers and the like; it is a medium of hostility to the stiffness, pomposity, artificiality and self-satisfaction into which people often fall.[29] This eschewal of final states and smug satisfactions is well shown by the concept of confession. In 1937 Wittgenstein made a series of confessions to close friends concerning past 'crimes' he had committed and which, weighed with guilt, he felt as a burden upon his soul[30] – it was a characteristic act for someone so concerned with showing and re-showing his place in the world. The urge behind these confessions was not a desire for sympathy, enclosure or forgiveness from his friends, nor the offering of explanations, reasons or justifications, nor an assertion of individuality, nor even an affirmation of the absolute power of those eliciting confession, but continual self-enactment and self-disclosure. Confession is a moment of overcoming, an evolution: a confession has to be part of your new life[31] and not an affirmation of established doctrines. Similarly, Foucault sees the process of confession, which he links to but radically develops from the Christian practice of penance and its role as signatory event in the visceral operations of sovereign power and torture,[32] as a technique of self-realization practised in the social world of institutional power circulation.[33] Confession involves the reaching of shifting equilibria between individual techniques of self-expression and institutional techniques of control and domination in the regime. The identity of people is an amalgam of the continued interplay between these related social forces; it is emblematic of a space defined by rules but which in definition encourages evasion. The role of confession is as an expression of an individual's power to decide for themselves, of how they are able to confess and learn from this act in the face of institutional control, of how once given life comes around anew and of how from the formal confessional itself new de-spatialized, 'smooth' lines of flight or 'unpredictable phrasings' come into perspective.[34] Such learning is perpetual – Wittgenstein's confession shows how this expression of power can be construed as moving confession from the grounding of the penitent to the grammatical. Penance for Wittgenstein was something approaching religious hypocrisy,[35] implying the attempt to replace one type of dogma, theory or ideology with another, a constant interplay of paradigmatic ideas, determinate conceptions of the good life. The motion, decision and learning identified by Foucault and encapsulated by Wittgenstein as grammatical is an expression of fluidity. Confession so conceived enables the individual to shed theories and dogma, or more accurately, to enable us to see them as such, rather than as things equating to or diverging from truth. Penance is the replacing of old garb with the new, conformism on the basis of revealed truth which, in a sense, manufactures what can be confessed to. We are penitent in the face of a received dogma which we have contravened and must make recompense for. It sets up a prescribed ideal towards which we must work, something we must become, such as a transcendental or communal self. Confession for Wittgenstein was not an attempt to re-gain lost equilibria, reveal truths or attain prescribed goals by filling out an ideal but a continual attempt to make oneself ones' own object, to face and re-face oneself. If this process amounts to a code of living it is one which calls for a subjectification and subjection manifest in both obedience and self-revelation and as such becomes a technique for living. Confession allows us to embrace our fallibility, to acknowledge that our identity is far from a stable, invariant self which must, so to speak, force its way into the institutional world, it invites us to *show* the power of resistance and belonging without invoking alternative codes.

Confession need not involve the overt, ritualistic and almost maso-
chistic laying bare of the soul to others which Wittgenstein felt necessary to purge his being of the vanity which he felt so often clouded
his judgement.[36] It can take more subtle, nascent but no less passionate forms where we attend to our efforts to bring about that which we
think is good in the face of temporary or more permanent dis-
appointment. It is the practice of trying to do what is right by ourselves in the context of adversity and achievement, which, above all
else, involves perpetual communication with others and our surroundings without presuming privileged positions or static aims. In
a passage reminiscent of Nietzsche Wittgenstein tries to convey the
strangeness of a self which seems replete or content in its being,
devoid of angst and disquiet:

> The way to solve the problem you see in life is to live in a way that
> will make what is problematic disappear.
>
> The fact that life is problematic shows that the shape of your life
> does not fit into life's mould. So you must change the way you live
> and, once your life does fit into the mould, what is problematic
> will disappear.
>
> But don't we have the feeling that someone who sees no prob-
> lem in life is blind to something important, even to the most
> important thing of all? Don't I feel like saying that a man like
> that is just living aimlessly – blindly, like a mole, and that if only
> he could see, he would see the problem?
>
> Or shouldn't I say, rather: a man who lives rightly won't experi-
> ence the problem as *sorrow*, so for him it will be a bright halo
> round his life, not a dubious background.[37]

Though at times this rejection of principles and theories on the ethics
of the human condition can cast us into solipsistic reflection,[38] it
encourages us to dispense with the illusion of calm that theoretical
constructions try and offer us; the rules we use in our lives 'do not
attempt to guide the totality of movements by prescription'.[39] Ordinary language is couched not in terms of salvation but in those of perpetual appropriateness and the opportunity such specific applications
offer us as they shift from moment to moment. The identity of people
becomes a conversation taking place at the points of confusion in our
relations with others, relations which are governed above all by
language. It is in language that our expectations and their fulfilment
potentially meet, in language that we create ourselves and are created
by our relations with others. It is through the self-referential (the
ability to examine oneself) and recursive (the ability indefinitely to

build and distrust linguistic meanings without necessary repetition) aspects of language that we as humans are able to envisage and criticize ourselves and our activities and accumulate, historicize and categorize the outcomes. In calling language ordinary Wittgenstein encourages us not to look beyond what we are. This focus on language and grammar allows us to make sense of how it is that many confusions result from the inevitable rasping occurring between ideal dogmas and practical experience; and of how human rights exemplify such a frictional generality by virtue of their conceiving of resistance and belonging as stable theoretical goals of a single regime of exchange, in rivalry with alternative regimes.

The trick of grammatical self-control is never to rest with established definitions, psychological states and the like. Human rights as certainties can and often do function not as remedies but as 'veils of ornamental deceit' which obscure the numerous different ways of solving problems of self-expression and control, many of which lie in the hands of indigenous peoples as opposed to the lofty tenets of international declarations. The genealogy, to use the concept in Nietzsche's sense, of human rights is characterized by flux and continual emergence, it is dialogic, yet most codes of human behaviour seem to remain solid, impersonal. This transcendental illusion which has concepts like human rights as invariant appendages to some inner, human core assumes an intellectual authority best exemplified by the uni-dimensional political utopias of Skinner (*Walden Two*) and Moore (*Utopia*) – a disturbingly uncontested, non-agonal human consensus in which language feels somewhat redundant; where everything has been said before and the only quality required is that one much feared by Mill, the ape-like virtue of imitation. Dogma, unshakeable conviction, is not just as something which determines opinion but which controls the *expression* of what constitutes opinion; it is prejudice to which everything *has* to conform.[40] Wittgenstein conceives it acting less like a wall setting limits to what can be believed, obvious in their physicality, but as a brake or weight which restricts movement,[41] which delineates the sense of legitimate resistance from manifest insanity. In being dogmatic, then, we are left like Malatesta's bandaged man, who believing his bound legs (which in this case signify the dictates of government) are actually what enable him to stand and move, resists any suggestion that he cut away the ties that bind and experiment with other ways of living for fear that he will never be able to move again.[42] For Malatesta certainty in political living often reduces us to little more than automata conforming with dominant significations.

Taking up a Wittgensteinian perspective, then, evokes the idea of a linguistic self, pivotal to which, as is well expressed by the practice of confession, is the ever-present responsibility for continuous choice: 'Concepts with fixed limits would demand a uniformity of behaviour. But where I am certain someone else is uncertain. And that is a fact of nature.'[43] What is of a phenomenal nature, then, is the *substantive* emptiness of setting limits; there is always the possibility of things being different. What this book attempts to show is how human rights are, from the perspective of language, better seen not as attempts to go back and re-establish old certainties nor to create new ones but as establishing formal conditions by which people can come to establish conditions, as limits, to their activity, a nexus of perspectives conceived *ordinarily*: not as patterns to be imposed but expressions of being in possession of that substantively indeterminate process called language[44] where what we think and what we are continually meet. As such ordinary human rights articulate the formal capacity to recognize the differences between things, to be constantly open to change and aware of the perpetual possibilities for error, learning, knowing, inventing, circulating and confession[45] as we push against the boundaries of language by virtue of our being in possession of the rules of that language. By resisting the temptation to construct or reveal ultimate knowledge[46] and postulating on tablets of stone politics, as the on-going institutionalized negotiation of creative language use, is well described by a conception of these rights, which make intelligible prospective lines of flight from the gravitational pull of common denominators, ideologies and truths whilst sustaining the embodiment of belonging through active and on-going confession. Improvements to our lives will never be brought about by the tinkering of social engineers, when what is required is for people to take control of their being and becoming in the here and now, and not for some abstract tomorrow or romanticized past. It is through this rejection of schematic spectacles, the reluctance to line things up in neat little rows like the medicinal bottles on the shelves of an apothecary, that ordinary human rights can come actively to promote confession rather than seek to impose and extend regimes of production and exchange. It is an apparent paradox that it is only by resisting such labels or names that one can get, through Wittgenstein, to a clear view of things, of how it is with the world.[47] His was an urge to get us to realize the differences between things, to see that belonging to groups and classes, including universal or species ones, often obscured rather than enhanced our relations with the world. The potential of confession is both a way of resistance to the alienating effects of such 'immutables' as unassailable ethical principles, absolute truths, relative truths and theories of everything and an affirmation of self weaving and re-weaving in a world with grammar.[48] Confession is of this world, and defines it.[49]

1 Private language . . .

We possess nothing in the world – a mere chance can strip everything – except the power to say 'I'. That is what we have to give to God – in other words, to destroy. There is absolutely no other free act which it is given to us to accomplish – only the destruction of the 'I'.

('The Self' in Siân Miles (ed.) *Simone Weil: An Anthology*, Virago, 1986, p. 99)

CONCEPTS AS PICTURES

Beginning with such perennial problematics as: 'How are we to harmonize the world with thought? How do we reconcile truth with its consideration? How do we know *what must be*?', Wittgenstein's early work conceived the answers as being revealed in logical form. Logic was the genesis and nemesis of meaning; outside of this form was silence. To *show* this (to prove or explain it would require analysis beyond logical form, which, given its omnipotence, was unintelligible) Wittgenstein envisaged the world being composed of things or objects, which were themselves unalterable, basic. 'Objects make up the substance of the world. That is why they cannot be composite.'[1] Only with objects can the world have an unalterable, subsistent form. These 'simples', what is 'unalterable and subsistent', combine to make up 'states of affairs' or 'complexes', 'what is changing and unstable.'[2] Facts, things, are not bare reality revealed, but constellations of objects[3] which occur within fields of logical possibility.[4]

Similarly, language is broken down into elementary words, or names, which combine to make up propositions. Words name things at the simple level and combine to form propositions in the same logical way as 'simples', or objects, combine to form the aggregate reality of states of affairs.

> Names are necessary for an assertion that *this* thing possess *that* property and so on.
> They link the propositional form with quite definite objects.
> And if the general description of the world is like a stencil of the world, the names pin it to the world so that the world is wholly covered by it.[5]

So language and reality are manifest through logic, 'the scaffolding of the world'.[6] Logic has no subject matter of its own, it is what allows us to describe and explain the world in the ways that we do through the unstable relationship between thoughts and propositions on one side and facts or things on the other.[7] Logic provides the space for notions of presence, being and all other ontological groundings.

So what there is and what there is not is determined by the totality of facts, facts being states of affairs or combinations of objects/things made possible through logical space which we represent through language. Words refer to objects, their worldly referents. The structure of language mirrors the structure of logical reality, just as a picture mirrors its subject. The emphasis here is upon *exemplary* logical structures rather than the *arbitrary denotation* of image. The mirroring is not a representation, or interpretation, but an expression of logical space.[8] Pictures made using language depict possible and non-possible states of affairs: 'We picture facts to ourselves. A picture presents a situation in logical space, the existence and non-existence of states of affairs.'[9] The limits of language are identifiable from *within* the pictures of objects. A picture does not depict its form or structure (form being the possibility that things are related to one another in the same way as elements of a picture are),[10] because it cannot stand outside of its exemplary *form*. In order to picture in the first place a picture must share with reality the logical form.[11] Thus: 'A picture represents a possible situation in logical space',[12] it is connected to reality 'like a yardstick'.[13] As such the things making up states of affairs as imitated by pictures are not factually distinct; they exist by virtue of their being set in relief against logical space.

The analogy of the divisionist painting style developed by Pissaro and Seurat helps bring out the crux of Wittgenstein's vision of a reality seen as a *logical composite* in which individual points or 'simples' have life. The divisionist technique was to construct a painting as an imitation of reality; as opposed to, say, an impression. This involved producing an image composed of tiny dots which in conjunction formed the constitutive elements of the tone. The closer one examines the image the dimmer becomes the overall effect, the states of affairs, and the more intense becomes the logical structure or form of those affairs, the dots, but these dots only have resonance by virtue of their conjunction with each other – outside of the image they would have no life. In painting this way Seurat and other divisionists were using precise and active description techniques to reveal what they felt was the formal harmony of the world. The sense of the painting represents the logical space of possible relations between things outside of which it is impossible to pass; it is the field of possibility. The tone of the image itself: the hues of colour; the light; the form; structure and the spatial setting; are what constitute the state of affairs, a meaningful whole. The divided image is composed of dots which are instances of logical space. This is very close to Wittgenstein's idea of the stuff of life, the 'simples'. 'In a picture the elements of a picture are the representatives of the objects.'[14] We do not normally recognize them as such; it is only upon close observation that such a logical structure behind the combined meaning, the overall image, is revealed. The dots in the painting, just like the 'simples' of reality, are situated in concert, in 'complexes', so as to create the images of the picture, the appearance of commonplace facts and states of affairs, but when deconstructed these dots and 'simples' are not phenomenally discrete, but logical possibilities which, if combined in different ways constitute a change in meaning – their presence would have a different resonance. In both cases the fundamental idea is that complex propositions or states of affairs are functions of simples, and because relations between states of affairs and facts actually transcend the facts or states of affairs themselves, language cannot say anything about its own relation with the world because its propositions are a picture of that world. Nothing can be meaningfully *said* about such relations; they cannot model the form of modelling. Propositions can describe reality but they cannot simultaneously explain how such description was arrived at without being self-referential, governed as they are by the logic of such descriptions.[15] Thus we reach the limits of language, the boundary of linguistic technique beyond which we are silent.

Words name things and propositions and sentences made up of those words reflect states of affairs made up of things; they reflect logical reality: 'a proposition is a picture of reality: for if I understand a proposition, I know the situation that it represents' and such knowledge is not something to be further supported or explained: 'I understand the proposition without having had its sense explained to me.'[16] To understand a language is to be embroiled in sense; its limits coincide with those of reality, they share the same logical form, the sense does not come from outside, but from an internal level whereby propositions represent states of affairs as actual ones in a field of all possible ones. Meaning is found in logic. If a proposition stands for a state of affairs whose configuration the logical relation models, it is true, and if it does not, it is false.[17]

This makes clear, then, that Wittgenstein was not advocating that the world was wholly open to scientific investigation, waiting to be uncovered by the employment of rational criteria, despite his connexions with Logical Positivism. In the *Tractatus* he equates the world, or reality, to a white sphere covered randomly with black dots over which Newtonian mechanical laws have placed a uniform mesh. It is the shape of the mesh which determines how it is we are *with* the world, it establishes the axioms of induction. Just as it is the fact that the sphere can be completely described by the net with a specific size of mesh, rather than the net itself, which tells us about the nature of the sphere, so it is that the laws of Newtonian mechanics tell us nothing about naked reality, but the *way* in which we are able to describe it in this way.[18] Laws relate to the net and not what the net describes, they are logically rather than physically contingent: 'The only necessity that exists is a *logical* necessity.'[19] People like the Logical Positivists were under the illusion that the laws of nature render plain descriptions of the world, an illusion because they failed to see that such a relation can only be shown, never defined as a foundation of knowledge.

In postulating the need for silence the *Tractatus* is, in some ways, a profoundly mystical work: in its making clear logical limits it constitutes a consideration of the beyond. In drawing limits to what can be expressed it delineates a realm to which there is an ineffable beyond, albeit one of no expressible sense, and this limit is, perhaps, the bounds of what is sayable, the *locus* at which values have their life. We can convey facts to each other through language, but the aesthetic and ethical flows cannot be represented as things, they are rendered unintelligible by such a mode of representation; what is of ultimate value can never be spoken of: 'It is clear that ethics cannot be put into words. Ethics is transcendental. Ethics and aesthetics are one and the same.'[20] Wittgenstein recognized that the mystical element in subjectivity, that which lies outside of the realm of questions, of use, and yet which imbues life with sense, can only be shown through the use of non-representational allegory and metaphor. The idea being suggested here is that in both art and ethics one sees

things in conjunction with everything else, rather than as situated in
everything else, such that:

> The work of art is the object seen *sub specie aeternitatis*; and the
> good life is the world seen *sub specie aeternitatis*. This is the con-
> nexion between art and ethics. Each thing modifies the whole
> logical world, the whole of logical space, so to speak. As a thing
> amongst things, each thing is equally insignificant; as a world
> each one equally significant.[21]

To adopt such dualistic notions of the world being eternally rent
between picture and non-picture, content and non-content, logic and
ethics, or fact and value required of Wittgenstein a tempered and
keen solipsism. Value is rendered explicit as a relation between God
and the 'I' which in no way denotes a thing; things only have signi-
ficance as being valuable by virtue of their relationship to the single
human will. The knowing self is not wholly of this world; it is both
constricted by and defining of the limits of this world, its world,
which is the only real world.

> This is the way I have travelled: Idealism singles men out from the
> world as unique, solipsism singles me out alone, and at last I see
> that I too belong with the rest of the world, and so on the one
> side *nothing* is left over, and on the other side, as unique, *the
> world*. In this way idealism leads to realism if it is strictly thought
> out.[22]

Thus the self does not belong to this world, it defines its limits – it is
the subject, and the subject alone, which could not be mentioned in
a book entitled *The World as I Found It*.[23] The world is the world
of the self, there is no distinction. Here Wittgenstein is talking not
of the body, or of psychological attributes, but of the metaphysical
self; the seat of the will which is independent of the world.

The world is a world of shape, of form, in which everything is as
it is, and in which nothing has value; if value exists it lies outside of
the world, outside of propositions, which can only picture the logical
form existing in the world. So value cannot be expressed in language;
the world is seen as the setting of the problems, not their solutions,[24]
which can only be found in non-propositional flights of imagination,
and personal leaps of faith. Any attempt to try and conflate fact
with value leads either to the distortion of facts through an imagination running with abandon, or to pronouncements of moral codes
which seek to control but which for Wittgenstein are nothing but
the bombast of ignorant onlookers in temples of silence and awe.

Ethics, like aesthetics, has nothing to do with the consequences or utility of action and everything to do with the action itself.[25] 'Good and evil', said Wittgenstein, 'only enter through the *subject*. And the subject is not part of the world, but a boundary of the world.'[26] Such a self is made manifest, it is mystical in that nothing can be said about it in philosophy or in science – it is the province of art, poetry and religion.[27] Toulmin and Janik, citing Wittgenstein's correspondence with Paul Engelmann as well as the *Tractatus,* see this focus on silence as indicative of Wittgenstein's wanting to show the poignancy of silence. His early work expresses an ethical point not in what it says but in what it omits.[28] The quest for the godhead of beauty, truth and goodness is not to be found in this world; this world is a symptom of those criteria adopted by the self in its world view; it is a world of change, of haphazard form whose movements cannot be explained as such. To see this world is to climb a ladder of insight, kick it away, and thence command a clear perspective of how things are with the world – contingent, fragmented, laughable, noisy, chaotic and bereft of a defined culture. To see the world aright is to acknowledge that nothing original can be said, only similes; to paraphrase Karl Kraus, to say something new is to step forward and be silent.

> If there is any value that does have value, it must lie outside the whole sphere of what happens and is the case. For all that happens and is the case is accidental.
> What makes it non-accidental cannot lie *within* the world, since if it did it would itself be accidental.
> It must lie outside the world.[29]

Ethics cannot be intellectualized; it is what is beyond contingency, it is that to which things are contingent – a semblance of will, part of a subject's attitude to the world. There is no metaphysical willing subject to be found in the world, no altar of human self upon which we are to set the icons of identity. To find will we must look outside of the world, to god, with the attendant risk that we may only see a void.

From the *Tractatus* emerges potentially shattering questions for the nature of ethical rules expressing relations between wills, like human rights. Either they are laws or principles and in that case, because ethics have no foundation, can only be prudential or useful guides to instrumental action; or they are expressive of an ethical aspect of will which cannot be spoken about *per se*. If the former then they cannot be absolute, inviolable nor universal, nor can they be ethical; human rights become nothing more than consequentialist tools of positive legal codes. If the latter then they cannot be laws but that which renders ethics to the realm of silence depictable not by natural law but solipsistic image, allegory and metaphor; they cannot be claimed, asserted, encoded, enforced or even spoken about. Concepts such as reward and punishment, the sense of duty, the knowledge of 'right' and good living, are wrapped up in the individual's will; they are terms for the concern of the individual alone:

> If the good or bad exercise of the will does alter the world, it can alter only the limits of the world, not the facts – not what can be expressed by means of language.
> In short the effect must be that it becomes an altogether different world. It must, so to speak, wax and wane as a whole.
> The world of the happy man is different from the world of the unhappy man. [30]

Ethics are deep-seated spiritual convictions about what is of value,[31] convictions which inform the world of content but are without content themselves. The happy person can inhabit the very same physical, economic and social space as the unhappy person and yet still occupy a different world, for *the sense of value* in the world is rendered not by any physical setting but by one's personal integrity, one's capacity to take the leap of faith into solipsistic communion with a form of the self-identity whereby in that nothingness, in that silence, one feels both great and small. Kierkegaard speaks of this feeling in his journals as the uniting of two great forces: humility and pride. It is an intensely private melding, a solitary reverie yielding a 'tranquil marriage of love', a rare experience of having

> found what the great philosopher – who by his calculations was able to destroy the enemy's engines of war – desired, but did not find: that archimedean point which for that very reason must lie outside the world, outside the limitations of time and space.[32]

What is good, of greatest sense, the riddle of life, lies in the outside.[33] Indeed so completely outside is ethics and aesthetics that nothing can be made of it, it is pure fantasy, so stable as to be free from any qualities whatsoever. There is an antinomy between art, ethics and life; between the spiritual structure or thought constructions (Schoenberg's tonal scale, Loos' *Raumplan*, Wittgenstein's solipsistic soul) and the spatial structures of logical and cultural forms.[34]

Human rights cannot, therefore, prescribe a specific ethical type, nor can they act as ethical laws, for laws assume a source of commonly agreed authority used to promote effective social relations, whereas Tractatan ethics are an entirely personal affair; they have nothing to do with punishment and reward outside of the action itself. The good life cannot be described; it is transcendental, a poetic ability to 'renounce the amenities of the world' which 'are so many graces of fate'[35] and to stand in silent occupation of an Archimedian point beyond logical form. This silence is brought about through a concern with purity in art. It is art that tugs at the complacency and deceits of the dogmatic, the theoretician and the warmonger; it is art which looks not to the multifarious effect but to the genesis; it is art which is agitated, vital, enchanted and inexhaustible, and it is art which engages with the immediate, the illiterate and the unknowable.

This reliance upon unique elements in unique situations can leave an impression of frustration amongst some commentators, like Koestler, who has said the *Tractatus* represents a decidedly queer juncture in philosophical reasoning – 'a man setting out to circumcise logic and all but succeeding in castrating thought'.[36] Human rights, as instances of ethical propositions, not only seem redundant in such a solipsistic world, they seem meaningless.

CONCEPTS AS DEEDS

Less a radical reversal of his thought constructions than a radical critique of such constructions *per se*, Wittgenstein's views on language developed significantly over the ensuing years, culminating in the publication of *Philosophical Investigations* in which he shows how what looks as if it had to be, the world as logical form, *only exists within a language*, and so by implication does the role of human will. No longer separate from but intimately and internally linked to its realization as action,[37] the will is conceived linguistically rather than metaphysically. What brings this change about is a reconsidered view on how language is used in the world.

Take what for Wittgenstein was a very illustrative case of language use – the role of the architect.[38] Under the *Tractatus* value system they would be artisans, craftsman in place and space meeting the material needs of human subjects, needs informed by the dominant values present within any one social tradition as it continues to flirt with and reassess its narrative past in order to sustain a balance between *the requirements* of inner and outer being. From this perspective architecture was a practical and imaginative response to prevailing trends in need, one articulated by Wittgenstein's Viennese acquaintance, the architect Adolf Loos.[39] Loos insisted on dividing the language of our needs and the practices which serve them, those of builders passing slabs to one another in order to construct, say, a shelter, from the language of our values, the same builders passing slabs to one another in order to construct, say, a mediæval cathedral. One is infused with sagacity, a conscious appraisal of what is useful, and the other is infused by a spirit of religious fervour; it has no practical purpose but glories in a faith which subsumes the vagaries of rain, frost and wind. For the cathedral builders 'The essential/was to perpetuate the force of their hope beyond the erosion of each season',[40] for a modern, anti-Secessionist architect like Loos the essential was to avoid the 'crime' of transposing ornament from alien cultures or engaging in self-conscious, wasteful and corrupting ornamental design. The architect, neither of rustic agrarian nor classical stock, should be respectful of continuity in culture by placing their services at the behest of a building's and its occupants' needs.[41] The architect was not a visionary, a revolutionary, but an exponent of comfort and function firmly set in the present. To see art as materially orientated is profane: art serves itself; it is private; it transcends condition; it is intimate with the spirit of the world; whereas architecture is imbued with the sentiments of time and place, and its job is to make those sentiments more precise.[42]

But this perspective, in eschewing as nonsensical an ideal language of 'wordless faith',[43] focuses upon the importance of *use* for architecture, on the need to 'jump into life so as to discover what man needs'[44] and in so doing must be aware that the architect, so obviously no longer a part of agrarian or craft culture but an urban bourgeoisie, cannot compensate by adopting either the purity of classicist line or a perfect functionalist sensitivity to felt need. To be beholden to cultural lineage, to be a part of established mores, practices and language was to realize that there could be no immutable division between art and craft, between purity and chaos, between the spoken and the unspoken; what was of function and what was of spirit varied with the circumstances of its articulation. Art was plastic, it was shaped by and shaped the spirit of the age, the ideal was such by virtue of its inhabiting a trend, everything was subject to language. Enchroaching upon Wittgenstein over the ensuing periods of his life was the realization that it was not the unsayable which existed beyond language, but that what was *beyond language* was still approachable through language and its conditions.

There is a very conscious move here from solipsism towards the view that language was an embodied and embodying activity understandable through grammatical reflection. Value, rather than being something mystical, allegorical and ineffable,[45] was in possession of its own *techne* whose rules could be described through objects of comparison. The *Tractatus*, whilst it emphasized self-disclosure and self-enactment as spontaneous expressions of our natural being, tended to suppress the need for 'a measure of collaborative human presence'[46] present in contextual roots, an institutional tutoring and awakening, an awareness of the need for a narratively based rigour of action which acknowledges that it must use, re-use, develop and destroy by working within and at the boundaries of whatever positions we find ourselves in. Solipsism itself is a grammatical perspective; instead of my language being the limits of my world, our languages becomes the limits of our worlds.[47]

The later work is still informed by the urge to make people see clearly that we can never explain everything, and that mystery will always remain; it is still infused with the pervading sense of chaos and uncertainty, but it is also infused with the realization that in order to posit any form of meaning, be it phenomenal or criterial, reference must always be made to the conditional space of regularity found in circulating norms, practices and narrative histories. The *Tractatus* was wrong not because it was a wrong theory but because all attempts to theorize in terms of absolutes and defining origins are doomed; their smoothness is conceived as distinct from, rather than relative to, the rough ground of ordinary language. Meaning is never complete and enclosed.[48] So naming something can only represent an *element* of reality;[49] it does not embrace the essence of what it is to mean or say something. Using concepts like colour samples[50] Wittgenstein tries to show the bewitching effect language can have on us when it is assumed that the subject/predicate form used in naming objects is imposed schematically upon language. It encourages the assimilation of what actually are different *uses* of words into the singular name–object form of the picture theory of language. Even in cases where they do name things, such as proper names, it does not get us far to say that, for example, the meaning of the United Nations is the body United Nations, or the meaning of the Declaration of Human Rights is the piece of paper upon which it is written, or part of the furniture of the universe. The picture naming theory employed the dual notions of reality, things-as-they-are, and language, things-as-we-see-and-name-them, and explored the relationship between the two; language explains or orders reality in this or that way and it does this best when it is in the logical form name–object.[51]

> One thinks that learning languages consists in giving names to objects. Viz., to human beings, to shapes, to colours, to pains, to moods, to numbers, etc. To repeat – naming is something like attaching a label to a thing. One can say that it is preparatory to the use of a word. But *what* is the preparation *for*?[52]

To better show this preparation Wittgenstein characterizes language in terms of games. Games have characteristics: they can be played with concentration using physical endurance and mental skill; they can be emotional; and they often require practice and dedication. But they can also be none of these things; there is no single common denominator to games distinguishing them from other practices. We learn what a game is according to contextual criteria, rather than rigid, sufficient and necessary conditions. Take the concept red, an oft-used term in Wittgenstein's investigations. In the majority of language games it is used as a colour – but this use gives rise to a myriad of possibilities which cannot be reduced to a single instance of the ultraviolet spectrum – for example: 'her face reddened' evokes not just colour, but feelings of embarrassment, or anger; 'nature is red in tooth and claw' requires an appreciation of violence; and very tangently Schoenmaeker's 'red is the mating of yellow with blue' or Klee's 'red is just blue screaming' require either an immersion in the vertical and horizontal orthogonal elements of the de Stijl movement or an embrace of emotional connectives with colour. In all these instances the grammar does not require that the uses of words maintain strict definitional relations with worldly referents because it itself is that world and not a commentary upon it. The absence of one set of features does not jeopardize the application of one term. There exist what Wittgenstein calls 'family resemblances' between the contexts in which the concepts 'red' and 'game' are used. Family resemblances establish coherence in language, they encapsulate the texture of words which are similar enough to ensure that their uses in language games criss-cross and overlap in many different ways but never in a sufficiently rigid manner to discern any essence in such games.[53] There is no one single common thread to them; they find stability by being wound round each other, like threads making up a fibre: 'and the strength of the thread does not reside in the fact that some one fibre runs through its whole length, but in the overlapping of those fibres.'[54] Meaning occurs as a family of use in a language;[55] non-linear and non-reducible.

To take the divisionist painting analogy again: along with much of the early modernist movement in art, divisionism was very consciously trying to reveal the skeleton of things, to get behind surface appearance so as to represent basic structures. Its statements are scientific, abstract and stable. As a result the paintings themselves are devoid of movement because they only attempt, as did the *Tractatus*, to render composite form. Seurat's pictures 'hang' in a two-dimensional, static plane; they do not reflect the partial, chaotic, tragic, emotional aspects of life. In a similar way the *Tractatus* can be seen as presenting a rarefied, abstracted view of a reality collapsed between sayable form and silent perfection, when really language can be made to do a lot more than speak in names.[56] Language is not used just to represent and explain, but also to report, to question, to persuade, to instil, to rebel, to exclaim and so on. Propositions do not just report new information and words and things do not have stable significatory relationships. One word does not mean just one thing, indeed things in themselves are never stable; there is no separate, immutable frame called logical space which defines the parameters of language; 'things' are always part of language. Reality is governed by a grammatical rather than formal logic. The structure of logical form was displaced by rules of language; rules which reflect both the inherent instability of things, even the very existence of things.

The divisionist aspiration to uncover the basic structures of the world using art as a representation could only ever offer an interpretation of a specific aspect of reality; that perspective framed by the reductionism of scientific methodology. Language does not have to limit itself to uncovering literal statements of fact, nor does art have to emulate this revelatory urge; meaning can be less tangible, emotional, an intuitive expression of feeling for which it would be ridiculous to seek support in terms of evidence yet which still retains a kind of weird sense because of the fluid capacity of grammatical forms.

CONCEPTS AS PRIVATE

Given the centrality of language to Wittgenstein it is helpful to dwell awhile on how it is we as language users are conceived. Ourselves, no less than any other thing, are equally enravelled in linguistic contexts – norms, practices, techniques and the like – and it is to these and not to some inner core that our identity is owed. Our tendency is to assume privileged status as agents – beings who somehow conjure up an identity which is then used to meet the world. This story is best, and most modestly, told by Descartes. The Cartesian self seems to float in its own bell jar, suspicious of the inevitably confusing, unreliable, doubtful and valueless substance in which it is immersed it retreats to the mirrored certainty of its own thought: the *cogito* – the always renewed event of thought: 'Myself who doubts, I think, I am, I am a thinking thing.'[57] I cannot doubt that I think and to think I must be. Doubt, thought and being (all of which are known by all by virtue of their doubting, thinking and being and hence require no pre-existing truth or knowledge) coincide to frame an entirely privileged first cause of self from which other objectivities can be drawn (e.g. one of my ideas is that of infinity, hence there must be a god) but none of which are epistemically prior to the *cogito*. Meaning, knowledge and understanding become mental certainties transferred from the inner to the outer by means of language, communication. They remain, then, uniquely attached to a doubting, thinking, being thing whose doubts, thoughts and states of being others can suppose (from reports, signs, etc.), but never actually know, not being the progenitor. All any of us can ever be sure about is our own feelings and experiences. This is the image of a private language which Wittgenstein rejects.

'What', asked Wittgenstein, 'gives us so much as the idea that living beings, things, can feel?'[58] How can we understand, for example, anothers' pain? Cartesian reasoning suggests we are unable to do this. But look at the role the ideas play in language games.[59]

> Look at a stone and imagine it having sensations. – One says to oneself: How could one so much as get the idea of ascribing a *sensation* to a *thing*? One might as well ascribe it to a number! – And now look at a wriggling fly and at once these difficulties vanish and pain seems to be able to get a foothold here, where before everything was, so to speak, too smooth for it.[60]

Pain gains a foothold here because of an appreciation of the context. The very idea of context is something which Cartesian reasoning casts into shadow, a murky and uncertain umbra of which we must be suspicious in the extreme. But to mistrust context is very strange indeed. If sensations were inherently private, if it is only from my own experiences that I know what it means to suffer, that I understand the experience of pain, then must it not be the case of everyone else too? But how can I reason about how it must be with others when I cannot make sense of their experiences?[61] That we clearly do extend considerations and attributes beyond the subject suggests that the isolate desolation into which the *cogito* is plunged by its own mistrust of the 'outside' is inherently problematic for any continuing sense in the world. The Cartesian is tempted into thinking that when we speak we are reporting on how things are within us; we are issuing responses which accompany the reality; we conceive of a split between the handling of signs and the understanding of these signs.[62] But for Wittgenstein a sense or feeling of pain does not accompany the sentence 'I am in pain' or any resulting pain behaviour, it is *part* of the very language. The exclamation 'I am in pain!' is recognized as part of the sensation of pain, sensations which people have been trained to use as a more refined and articulate replacements for crying, writhing or uttering a moan, which still have their place in the language game and which extend to children, the mute and even animals. To recognize pain in others, then, is not to see the entity pain and the entity subject and describe their capacities, for there are no such separate entities, but to see *that* someone is in pain. This is a

> grammatical [remark], not [a] statement about the observational limitations of the human beings in respect of the mental . . . any more than the claim that one's left hand cannot give one's right hand a gift exhibits a peculiar set of (physical?) limitations on the range of human behaviour.[63]

The idea is that we understand pain; *given certain criteria*, I can be as certain of pain as of any fact.[64]

> Consciousness in another's face. Look into someone else's face, and see the consciousness in it, and a particular *shade* of consciousness. You see on it, joy, indifference, interest, excitement, torpor, and so on. The light in other peoples' faces.
>   Do you look into *yourself* in order to recognize the fury in *his* face? It is there as clearly as in your own breast.[65]

Language is learnt and understanding is assessed in accordance with a developing sensitivity towards and mastery of language games (facial shades) none of which are linked to fixed psychological states as Descartes conceived them. Pain, like all concepts, has many uses, manifestations[66] (the agonized cry, the facial contortion, the resigned shrug, the quiet desperation, the longing gape, etc.) in many different contexts.[67]

It is a mistake, says Wittgenstein, to see language as just reporting our inner sensations because *what* we feel and *how we express* what we feel are *part of us*, our being, and feelings are not limited to sensations alone – they encompass emotions which cannot be pointed to, located and identified in themselves. There are reasons for emotions and causes of sensations which cannot be isolated from the sensations themselves,[68] whereas the Cartesian views inner experience and feeling as caused by some antecedent event or memory of an event. When Rousseau collapsed under an apple tree and began to weep inconsolably being, as he was, in a state of utter despair about the condition of his world, the world was not the cause of his grief but its object. He grieved *about* something, not *because* of something.

Imagine, says Wittgenstein, being a solitary individual who, anxious to speak, records sensations in a diary so as to remember their occurrence and what names they gave them. They create their own rules: for this sensation of pain they use 'Arghh', for that one they use 'Ow', and then follow them in the future. The problem with this notion of a private language lies not only in its assumption that such things as anxiety, diaries and the practice of using them already exist, but also in the complete inability to separate following a rule, that which governs correct identification of a feeling, from thinking they have followed a rule, the feeling of correct action. It renders the speaker weird, useless; 'it is humiliating', remarks Wittgenstein, 'to have to appear like an empty tube which is simply inflated by the mind'.[69] If a language was essentially a private affair then the resulting vacuum of contextual reference means we can make any action or feeling accord with a rule, relying as we do upon nothing more than self-referential inner memory – an act of authorization which for Wittgenstein seems as bizarre as picking up copies of the same newspaper to check that what it said was in fact the case. The mind believes it has access to evidence which it uses to check the correctness of its following a rule – it accords with the instance in the diary, but this belief is fallacious; the evidence does not exist, it is nothing other than the mind confirming itself, which is no confirmation at all. When the 'diarist' uses 'Ow', for example, does it refer to a pain in the shoulder, a dull pain, a long-lasting pain, a fake pain, a pain felt on the full moon, a grievous pain? There is no possibility of being sure; external checks of memory are unavailable, there only being access, in terms of meaning, to what is private. Thus, 'to *think* one is obeying a rule is not to obey a rule. Hence it is not possible to obey a rule "privately": otherwise thinking one was obeying a rule would be the same thing as obeying it'.[70]

How, then, is it possible for us actually to come to regular instances of meaning? If we cannot rely on the private sphere of mind, what can we rely on as a 'court of appeal'? There are two issues at stake here. Firstly, the role of context in meaning. To speak a language is to follow established techniques, procedures and contingent rules which determine good from bad, correct from incorrect and truth from error. In knowing something we are immersed in established ways of doing things. Ignorance is something relative to the conditions of its articulation. 'Whether I know something depends upon whether the evidence backs me up or contradicts me. For to say one knows one has a pain means nothing.'[71] Here the knowledge of something like pain taps into a narrative heritage which would arise from a sense of primitive sympathy for the plight of others, Rousseau's *pitié* or the good Samaritan in us all,[72] and extend in many ways depending on what over time has come to constitute the norms of pain criteria. Pain judgements are reached against a background set of conditions.[73] Experiences are defined by criteria, not by things, criteria which are not just outward manifestations of behaviour, but part of a logical grammar rooted in the specific contextual schemes belonging to its use.[74]

The pervading influence of circumstance leads on to the second issue: whether it is right to accept instances of pain as a problem of knowledge at all. That pain ascription requires a body of understanding, evidence and assessment to be determined in each instance by some form of checking procedure which sets it in relief against established contexts does not necessarily invoke claims to legitimated, proven or adjudged correctness. Evidence has no sense at the level of understanding – it is, indeed, only sensible to appeal to evidence once it is established we agree in some regular form or other, once we go by the practice of making appeals to methods of adjudication in the first place.

CONCEPTS AS UNIVERSALS

These issues arising from the private language argument consign universal, ethical principles like human rights to an uncertain and contextually dependent existence. The Tractatan view left human rights almost meaningless; the description of what it would be to live in possession of a formally private language leaves them almost biteless. The foundational paraphenalia of human rights discourse – the rational core of worth, the self-willing subject, the isolate decision-maker, the universal or natural law, and the ethical primacy are all jeopardized by the private language argument and its insistence that to have any sense or conceptual grip requires of us a tethering in actual conditions of being, conditions which are neither universal not atomized, but aspects of the whole hurlyburly of human activity.

That grammar circumscribes activity in the ways it does suggests that human rights, as grammatical units, only have meaning to those language users who have learnt the relevant techniques and purposes of their application. They have no bite beyond their agreed application. They become merely confirmatory. Even if it is supposed that people are essentially choosers before being defined by what they have chosen, this can only ever be a belief, a contextual, culturally bound practice or tradition with limits in its use and without recourse to abstract justification. Human rights are icons of humanistic myth – a functional, a valuable myth for sure – but a myth all the same, one which arises out of customs and traditions of the social weal and not from the divine machinations of the universal *Geist*. Ethical development is a specific experience invoking existing grammatical criteria[75] where we dispense with meta-narratives and explain dignity, respect and worth as grammatically framed intentions. Our Western, democratic community requires that we treat people in an open, tolerant and respectful manner and that is just it, that is how we do things, that is part of our web of beliefs, conventions and purposes. This is not to say that human rights collapse into materially orientated utilitarian fixtures[76] which, in the words of Herbert Spencer, give 'formal sanction and better definition to those assertions of claims and recognitions of claims which naturally originate from the individual desires of men who have to live in the presence of one another'.[77] But in having moral import they remain perspectival – they can no longer be universally valid codes of being – their legitimacy lies with their use as site-specific value judgements.

Wittgenstein's private language argument attacks our temptation to dignify ourselves as isolated bestowers of value and understanding. It also gives rise to the ensuing problem of if not the 'I' then what? If the subject is not the root of all understanding and knowledge then what is? This in turn provokes considerations as to whether context or circumstance act as alternative bedrocks upon which structures of knowledge can be built by those inhabiting such periods and places. That the shift in Wittgenstein's philosophy was crucially orientated around a concern to dissolve the rigidity of structures in terms of their being absolutes suggests the role of context is not so arbitrary and relativistic as may be suggested if the private language argument is read as replacing the non-intelligible appeal to memory with an appeal to contingent circumstance. It is the opacity as well as the surety which Wittgenstein investigates in his concern with how concepts like pain and red and understanding are used. So doubting the existence of pain, for example, does not arise just because doubt is the only thing of which we can be sure; but nor does it arise just because the pain behaviour fails to conform with established instances of such behaviour. Because people fail to wear their pain on their sleeves does not necessarily mean they are not in pain.[78] That doubt arises, then, is through continuing encounters with inappropriate instances of use, use which invokes the spirit as well as the form of the rules governing pain.

It is in discerning the ways in which inappropriateness is conceived that Wittgenstein is engaged here. He eschews any dualistic perspective which has on the one side a view of external objective reality which lends our pursuits and actions purpose and which determines truth and falsity (empirical realism or idealism), and on the other an indirect reality as we know it through our customs, accident and inter-subjective[79] agreement (a position espoused by various philosophical positions such as sensationalism, relativism and anti-realism).[80] To partake of this dualism is to not follow through the private language argument where meaning is construed in terms of sense, and not in terms of what is true and false in reality. Appropriateness concerns sense and intelligibility, not knowledge.

So in using a language we are creatures who are confined in some way or other to the temporality of a present arising out of an historical past and envisaged possible futures. This is a state of ordinary language, opaque rather than visionary, and one of which we should be aware if we are to avoid the confusions consequent upon envisaging concepts, rules and being as one thing.

> Philosophers who say: 'After death a timeless state will begin', or 'at death a timeless state begins', do not notice that they have used the words 'after' and 'at' and 'begins' in a temporal sense, and that temporality is embedded in their grammar.[81]

It is how sense arises from this temporality and spatiality of condition that shows how meaningful talk, if any, of ethical rules and practices is to proceed.

2 ... public rules

[L]anguage wells up in an enigmatic multiplicity which must be mastered.

(Michel Foucault *The Order of Things*, Tavistock, 1970, p. 305)

Wittgenstein's early distinction between fact and value consigned ethical principles, which had no referent, to an entirely subjective unity of being-in-itself which could never be explained or justified but only made apparent through personal integrity.[1] The ethical self delineates the world, it does not act within it, and each world has unique resonance by virtue of this Lutheran isolation. This mental reservoir, a solipsistic generator of value, was radically re-configured in Wittgenstein's later work into a self in possession of grammar whose contingency meant the idea of any truth foundation to ethical practices by which they may be guided was nothing but an emblem of confusing and arrogant error. Language was no longer connected through image to logical form; it was embedded in rules of use followed by the language users. In *Philosophical Investigations* understanding becomes a shared social activity, a publicly defeasible act of conformity with the norms of existing practices which themselves, being the arbiters of what is correct and incorrect in terms of sense, are beyond meta-ethical reproach. The only possible engine of change in ethical perspective was a momentous and populous switch in attitudes brought about by shifts in conceptual use themselves dependent upon relations with conditional, grammatical logic. In such circumstances ethics is prone to hibernate; set to wake only with the greatest of agitation it adopts a ponderous, chthonic state of being.

Such is the conservative rendering of Wittgenstein's later work. But there is much in *Philosophical Investigations* and his other collected remarks which erodes such an interpretation. Though Wittgenstein's concepts of rule, form of life, family resemblance, language game and natural facts reveal a sympathy with and an appreciation for what might be called the established politics of living, within their formulations lies an urge to clarify which has far from filial implications when it comes to the examination of social institutions. The gist of the later work is that though linguistic meaning comes to be determined by intra-linguistic rules rather than through a logical form shared by language and reality, this is as much a critique of cultural *carte blanche* as it is of scientific or logical realism. Wittgenstein's ideas on linguistic and grammatical rules see language and meaning internally linked through aspects of sense which are not imposed but the result of the reciprocal awareness of language in the recursive and self-referential activity of dialogue. Language, as Wittgenstein conceives it, is very much a motion, a vibrancy, an ongoing and shifting engagement with myth made possible by commitment to the rules of such myth; it is to the nature of these rules and their context that this chapter is devoted.

RULES AND CRITERIA

The private ostensive definition required by a private language presupposes already existent grammatical practices, a stage setting without which rules of language would just 'hang in the air', devoid of any meaning because they were unable to establish any regularity in use. Language is the regular *use* of sounds/words/gestures/hints *in specific contexts*; contexts which establish regularity in use through criterial or representational rules which determine how it is we are to proceed if we are to follow this or that language game. Such regularity is rule-based, and so it is through rules that language lives. There exist, according to Wittgenstein, criteria which show us a person does not understand a word, criteria for thinking he understands the word, though he does not, and, lastly, criteria for his correct understanding.[2] 'In the second case', says Wittgenstein, 'one might speak of subjective understanding. And sounds which no one else understands but which I *"appear to understand"* might be called a private language.' The subjective second case is distinct from the criteria for correct understanding, the third case, because appearing to understand necessitates checks of memory which in actual language use do not go on, there being no way to ascertain the correctness of one's memory without relying on something external to it, which then has to rely on something beyond it, *ad infinitum*. Misunderstandings are part of language use. Rather, Wittgenstein is trying to show that the only way of moving beyond misunderstandings is through criteria which establish sense. To establish sense is not to forage for external checks, but to show how certain criteria act as an internal connexion between understanding and its expression.[3] This internal link forges the foundation of grammar whereby the link between a rule and its application also becomes, as G. Baker and P. Hacker point out, an internal one: 'The foundations of language are not in private experience, the given "indefinables", but in normative regularities of conduct.'[4] We understand a rule by following a rule, we do not first understand and then follow. For a rule to be part of a language there must already be an element of sense and meaning built in to its use, its expression.[5] If a rule is understood, if it is grasped, then it must be *applied in a certain way*, a way we are taught to follow as part of our regular action. Rules enable by virtue of their criterial aspects; we have internalized the rule as 'my *last* court of appeal for how I am to go'.[6]

How am I supposed to follow a sign post if whatever I do is a way of following it?
But, that everything can (also) be *interpreted* as following, doesn't mean that everything is following.
But how then does the teacher interpret the rule for the pupil? (For he is certainly supposed to give it particular interpretation.)
– Well, how but by means of words and training?
And if the pupil reacts to it thus and thus; he possesses the rule inwardly.[7]

Rules are those indications which point out where it is possible for us to move about within our language; they govern the techniques and purposes of our grammatical actions.[8] They do not force us to play certain language games, we can choose to follow rules, not so choose, or create new rules, but in so changing the rules we inevitably change the meaning of our activity because of the internal link between understanding and following a rule. The *criteria* of correctness infuse our interpretations of meaning; interpretations alone cannot render something meaningful.[9] Meaning does not lie behind the use of a rule and determine its occurrence but is manifest in these criteria which we do not continually interpret but just grasp. An act of understanding is not forced; it is an expression of criterial familiarity, habit, established technique and custom by which people are guided.[10]

A rule is best described as being like a garden path in which you are trained to walk, and which is convenient. You are taught arithmetic by a process of training, and this becomes one of the paths in which you walk. You are not compelled to do so, but you just do it.[11]

Rules generate their own authority through criteria – to play this game you must follow these paths, and in so playing they compel us one way or another,[12] and the compulsion is akin to that we feel when following a path; it allows us to function. Stuart Shanker sums this up as follows: 'Although the actual existence of a rule may, so to speak, be dependent upon us, the 'truth' of the rule is dependent upon the rule itself.'[13] A rule shows me what I must do[14] and the must is nothing more than the inexorableness of an attitude towards techniques.[15] A rule is a sign for us always to do the same. 'The employment of the word "rule" is interwoven with the employment of the word "same".'[16]

Understanding rules, what constitutes the same, is not a single process which we can point to and describe, an established entity which repeats itself inside our minds. The fact that we describe the process misleads us into seeing it as a single, identifiable experience. 'But', says Wittgenstein, 'we forget that what should interest us is the question: how do we compare these experiences; what criterion of identity do we fix for their occurrence?'[17] The reasons for why things happen, the explanations given of the meaning of words, the descriptions of sensations, these are possible because of the criteria within which we undertake to consider them. 'What determines our judgements, our concepts and reactions, is not what *one* man is doing *now*, an individual action, but the whole hurly-burly of human actions, the background against which we see any action.'[18] What distinguishes action from non-action is not anything non-linguistic but the criteria by which the concept makes sense, its roles in language[19] linked by family resemblance. When we see someone raise a hand this can be gestural familiarity, a response to a question, an indication of identity, an involuntary spasm, a controlled experiment and so on. Whether it constitutes an action, and which type of action, depends upon the criterial context. It is in this sense that language is the vehicle of understanding;[20] we can urge ourselves to try to understand, but we cannot urge ourselves to understand without first accepting the criteria by which we classify what makes sense.

This point is made clear by Michel Foucault who, in *The Order of Things*[21] talks of a Chinese encyclopaedia which classifies animals into a bizarre taxonomy which includes categories for: animals looking like suckling pigs; animals drawn with a fine camel-hair brush; frenzied animals; and animals which from a long way off look like flies. Such a system, far from being absolutely natural and secure, has resonance from within the criteria of established linguistic practices. The point is being made that classificatory systems do not reflect things as they are *alone*; they are internally related to the concept of thingness, such that it can in certain, admittedly unusual, circumstances be bestowed on any of the above. Conditions of possibility reside in linguistic continuums and imprecisions concerning the identification of thresholds between language games. Criteria act gravitationally – the more exploratory the use of concept, the less pull has the conditional locus, and the greater the possibility of pulling away from one gravitational field to another. Classifying renders constant the totality of representations of the world – but things and words are interwoven here – things reside in language yet lend language the continuum which is the condition of its possibility.[22] Western taxonomy is a fusion of objects and criteria, as is well shown by Keith Thomas,[23] who describes the move from the anthropocentric systems of classifying nature, for example the naturalist Buffon's classification of animals into edible and inedible, the tame and the wild, the useful and the useless, or Aristotle's division of animals in terms of human characteristics such as mean or generous, noble or cowardly, to a more 'scientific' system of classification, for example the Linnaean plant classification which looked at the internal structure of stamens, pistils, etc. to determine relative positions within the framework. What constitutes what thing shifts with the sands of narrative time.

So for Thomas as for Foucault natural history cannot be disassociated from language; even the threshold of life itself is criterially governed:

> It is usual to divide the things in nature into three classes: minerals which are recognized as capable of growth, but not of movement or feeling; vegetables, which are capable of growth and are susceptible to sensation; and animals, which are capable of spontaneous movement. As for life and the threshold it establishes, these can be made to slide from one side of the scale to the other, according to the criteria one adopts.[24]

This linguistic conditionality is not an exercise in paradigm repetition; the relations between nature and grammar established through criteria are both inclusionary and critical; ordinary language is used and worked upon in order that alternative denominations be given. This critical relation has an established aspect of resemblance, where the classification works towards conceptual schemes of identity and existence validated against a background of sensory perception, and an emerging aspect of radical critique, where classification of life points to a consideration of being, a shift from the focus on conceptual clarity and representation through naming, to one which questions the ideas of representation, being and proposition themselves.[25] Between these aspects then there are possible shifts not only in what is called or identified as life, but in what life itself is. In adhering to criteria the language user invokes a *type*, a conditional and contested framework which is both used and, at least potentially, challenged through use – what is a type is what is created.[26]

Grammatical logic embraces the possibility of such shifting perspectives on criteria. Wittgenstein is trying to make us aware of the difference and vitality as well as the certainty experienced in language and how prone we are, when investigating things, to hide this by invoking and seeking to sustain formulae, definitions, blueprints and the like. That language has no essence,[27] that there is nothing universally common to any language game revealing a definite structure for language, is suggestive of potential as much as restriction. 'We remain unconscious of the prodigious diversity of all the everyday language games because the clothing of our language makes everything alike. Something new (spontaneous, "specific") is always a language game.'[28] Wittgenstein likened our use of language to wandering around a city with its different quarters, its moods, its thoroughfares, its very motion, all of which is contained, but by criteria and not absolutes or universals. Grammatical criteria always remain under-determined for there is no complete set of rules for employing all words in all instances. We follow rules much like we follow the signs which guide us through a city – they are enabling patterns as opposed to ones of imposition. 'The regulation of traffic permits and forbids certain actions on the part of drivers and pedestrians; but it does not attempt to guide the totality of their movements by prescription.'[29] The ideal ordering of grammar, like of traffic, is nonsensical.

RULES AND FORMS OF LIFE

Rules foster coherent and consistent human activity. Take Mondrian's picture *Boogie Woogie Broadway* – though composed of horizontal and vertical lines the image is one of life, the iridescent blobs of colour moving up, down and across the canvas are the city in motion, moving from place to place, resting, just being. Even reduced to its bare nuances New York City buzzes with life. Rules are used like this. But how is it we *actually do follow them*? We may be pleased as a species with certain rhythms, harmonies, proportions and relations but are these just a matter of accident, a fortuitous whim of the creator? Rules guide us like 'signposts',[30] but how do we recognize these posts as signs – and not, say, as giant toothpicks or religious totems. As Wittgenstein himself recognizes: 'A person goes by a sign-post only in so far as there exists a regular use of signposts, a custom.'[31] So following a rule requires more than the rule itself; there are criteria for training, technique, learning and mastering the form of a rule which are grammatical, but not mere instances of rule.

This investigation was well posed by Wittgenstein for himself at §437 (*Philosophical Investigations*) – 'Whence', he asks, 'this *determining* of what is not yet there. This despotic demand?' How is it that we already know what will satisfy a thought, an intention or a correct rule following procedure when those things are not even there, when we have not as yet experienced them, when we have as yet to follow the path suggested? How an intention to act links with what it is intention of, and how a rule links with its being followed is not solved by reference to the mental model of the Cartesian or to the picture model of the *Tractatus*, for these merely shift the issue about,[32] but nor can it be shown purely by reference to rules alone, for to follow rules itself presupposes stage setting.

Wittgenstein avoids these problems, all in some way indicative of a fetishistic temptation constantly to explain through reductionism,[33] by reference to a *natural consensus in judgements and actions*[34] manifest in our intentions to act being in agreement with our actions themselves – it is a consensus of grammar and hence remains internally linked to our action; it is not an external cause or justification. There is a regular connexion between the uttering of a sentence, a resultant action and the occurrence of that state of affairs that brings the purpose of the action about which somehow *just is*. We can only follow our intentions beyond the present, a rule can only determine its outcome in advance, if these rules are accepted as *a matter of course*. Although seemingly unsatisfactory this answer, if answer it can be called, for as will be seen it is not a state of knowledge, is clarified by Wittgenstein in his concept 'form of life':

'So you are saying that human agreement decides what is true and what is false?' – It is what humans *say* that is true and false; and they agree in the *language* they use. That is not agreement in opinions but in form of life.[35]

Taking, as Wittgenstein often did, an example of primitive learning in which the techniques of learning become illuminating in their obliqueness, language becomes a motion of initiation from within this form of life.

> If one of a pair of chimps scratched the figure # in the earth and thereupon the other the series ### . . . the first would not have given a rule nor would the other be following it.
> If, however, there were observed, for example, the phenomenon of a kind of instruction, of shewing how and of imitation, of lucky and mis-firing attempts . . . if at length the one who has been so trained put figures one after the other in sequence as in the example, then we should probably say that one chimp was writing rules down, and the other was following them.[36]

We are, in short, versed in the practice of rule following by a training which involves instruction on and familiarization with the idea of purposes, points, aims *per se*. A language game can only be grasped by someone immersed in the techniques of rule following learnt from playing other games.[37] We can follow a rule and yet still end up like Goethe's sorcerer's apprentice following the procedure of the spell but utterly confused as to the point, purpose and techniques involved in the context of application. We understand rules by virtue of our perspective from a form of life, the wider context of language use, the system of grammar which *establishes the possibility of showing* what is to count as correct and incorrect.

In being taught techniques we are educated in looking at things in ways which are given – we are shown connexions which are rigid, and so much linguistic activity involves turning one's back on rules in use; we follow the direction without hesitation.[38] Such an inexorability consists in their being an important part of our lives, techniques we employ over and over again 'with endless practice, with merciless exactitude'. These cannot be said to be true; to be true is to say 'that this follows from that' and the rigidity of 'that' is found in use, and whatever 'that' is can only be established by criteria; it is only through criteria that we can get into conflict with, or even conceive of, truth.[39] Proof of its being correct requires nothing more than its replication – there is nothing behind so to speak. The reality that 'correct', 'true' or 'right' accord with is a conventional perspective, a use which somehow forces itself upon us, which strikes us by virtue of our training.

However, it is how this 'turning of our backs' is established without being merely passive or even stupid that remains in question, how we come to learn our first instance of playing a game – notably as to whether it involves or invokes an appeal to a multiplicity of *agents* manifest in some form of community agreement[40] (it is community which decides what is to count as certain, as a game), or is something which remains confined to the multiplicity of *actions*[41] (it is our natural potential for regular game-playing behaviour which is the seat of certainty). Whether we avoid the 'problem' of philosophical regression in the interpretative paradox of §198 (*Philosophical Investigations*) (if individual interpretation was the basis of correctly or incorrectly following a rule then any action could be made to accord with any rule and thus following a rule would be indistinguishable from thinking one was following it), by virtue of communal dictat or because of a rhythm or regularity which is part of our natural history, is a critical problem in any attempt to tease out political implications from Wittgenstein's work. If the former then subjects would be little more than cultural puppets, prisoners of rule following systems over which they have little perspective; whereas if Wittgenstein is alluding to the latter, the concept of certainty is less an established system than a resonance established by criteria which we tend towards but which in no way acts as a judge and jury over our actions. It is the nature of the 'yardstick' by which what counts as doing the same gets its motive force that requires clarifying here.

In digesting Wittgenstein's comments on rule following it seems clear that in the distinction between one chimp copying another in a regular series and one chimp following another after instruction, mistakes and so on, there is an awareness that language requires more than just *behavioural* regularity in action. Although it is possible to envisage rules which only require such regularity, linguistic rules are not of this type; they are normative and involve established sanctions.[42] Rules guide our conceptions of a situation in accordance with norms – they have conditions of success or failure built in. We follow a path *to or from* somewhere. Clearly, to speak a language is to take part in a practice involving techniques and normative purposes with a specific narrative history.

The problem with equating such regular narrative conditions with the empirical precedent[43] of community standards which is to act as some form of supra-language game yardstick by mediating between correct and incorrect rule following is that,[44] as Baker and Hacker point out, this reduces following a rule to acting in accordance with an empirical majority which exists independently of, and hence in some quasi-causal relation with, each individual action. Rules and their extensions have to be related *internally*. Just like the link between intending and knowing what will fulfil my intention is an internal one, so the understanding of a rule cannot be separated from the knowledge of what constitutes a correct application of it. To separate them is to re-admit dualist confusions arising from attempts to analyse how it is that the two connect, or how the individual action 'represents' the correct one.

> *Given that there is* a certain rule, then nothing other than the rule constitutes the standard of correctness. In particular, it is misconceived to argue that *this* act does not accord with *this* rule because most people would not act in this way when given this rule . . . *Contra* Russell, nothing mediates between a desire and what counts as its satisfaction, or between an order and what counts as fulfilling it. So too, community agreement does not mediate between a rule and what counts as accord with it.[45]

It is not the community but the rule which acts as a standard of correctness, nothing stands between the rule and action.[46]

In *Zettel* Wittgenstein asks himself the very same questions about community agreement in response to how it is we judge that we have paid attention in establishing correctly an inner ostensive definition:

> But isn't human agreement essential to the game? Must not anybody who learns it [the definition] first know the meaning of 'same', and do not the pre-suppositions of this include agreement? and so on.[47]

> To say this is red, how do we know, is it only by human agreement?[48]

The answer is that it is wrong to search for any answers here; conceiving the issue as a question of the role of community agreement is acting like 'viewing by inspection', something which implies that in addition to the process of looking or seeing there is an external process of 'turning round' to check and see if such a view is correct,[49] whereas we do not speak in such a way. Language is not something which is connected to our lives and speaking it does not involve us in a continual motion of checking the correctness of our utterances and actions *against* some one background community agreement.[50]

We are taught to make certain moves, to give certain descriptions, but the flow of activity has no ultimate court of appeal; no final expression that this is what constitutes following this rule.[51] It is true that rules only exist when there is an established practice, an historical component, but, say Baker and Hacker, this practice which constitutes the framework of a rule need not be agreed upon in some form of inter-subjective communion, though it must be shareable (have the potential to be a *social* practice) in that others may come along and understand it, because of its regular nature. To be intelligible a rule must be understood as showing a normative regularity, as being translatable.[52] But the authority generated by this rule is not necessarily legitimated by a community, though it can be taken up and codified by one; it is internal, an aspect of what it is to behave intelligibly, and hence guiding, but in an under-determined way[53] whereby its force, its path, is used to see, act or be and not to confirm.

Wittgenstein was wary of any appeal to grounds of objectivity, of any claim either within the community or in some transcendental realm to certain knowledge. What we must concern ourselves with is how it is we come to understand each other, a question which is not empirical or epistemological but grammatical. Language is grammatically bound with the possibility of sharing judgements, but not with its actuality. Wittgenstein was not saying that language could not be spoken alone, but that it was not in the nature of language to be essentially private. Following rules involves us in ascribing mastery of a technique, and such mastery may be found in the behaviour of a solitary person, whether they have been a member of a community or not.[54] Regularity rests on some form of agreement – but it is not an empirical, contractual mode of reasoning, rather agreement at the level of forms of life which ensures that the majority in the majority of cases behave in an intelligible manner.[55]

Understanding in *Philosophical Investigations* comes to be seen as a process of increasing involvement with the technique of application of rules and of acquaintance with the purposes and techniques of the activity itself. It is in forms of life that we come to grasp the meaning of subtle glances, hints and movements, what Wittgenstein terms the 'imponderable evidence'[56] that goes to make up language. The agreement in judgements is quiet, unobtrusive, and represents a condition of use of concepts like mistake, truth, correctness, lie and so on – it is the form of life which provides the conditions within which normative ascriptions have life.[57]

RULES AND CERTAINTY

The form of life acts somewhat like Kant's categories here;[58] without these felt convictions of agreement and regularity understanding, indeed what it is to be recognizably human, would become an impossibility. It delineates the condition of human relations and as such is not something which requires explanation. The form of life acts as a criterion of being. Our relation to the world here is not one of knowing, but of belief and being – for knowledge itself is predicated on its resonance, hence its limits could not be described as perfect, absolute or true.[59] Without this given condition rules become nothing more than lines in shadow going from nowhere to nowhere. Rules require a non-epistemic certainty of being in a world-with-language; without this tether it is not just that a paranoia of isolation would quickly ensue, but that isolation itself would collapse into dissolution. 'For language games to persist it's essential that doubt is impossible at certain points.'[60] Or 'Doubting and non-doubting behaviour. There is the first only if there is the second.'[61] Doubt is logically excluded from the domain of propositions in the sense that to believe anything we must first be committed to a whole system of propositions which give mutual support to the process of linguistic activity. Activity: a system of conviction within which all doubting and accepting takes place. The myth carries with it the capacity to impress, to secure trust; to permit gestures, assertions, claims and convictions to be expressed and acknowledged, 'it belongs to the essence of what we call an argument. The system is not so much the point of departure, as the element in which arguments have their life.'[62] When we are compelled by a proof, say, in mathematics, we are able to go ahead in such-and-such a way, and refuse any other path. All I should say as a final argument against someone who did not want to go that way, would be: '"Why, don't you see . . . !" – and that is no *argument*.'[63] It is an expression of a proof which is a convention, perhaps linked to practical requirements, which is in no way an empirical proposition. The grammatical nature of meaning necessitates that belief comes before doubt. Wittgenstein, as Shanker has said, is trying to take us away from the realist–anti-realist pictures of meaning, both of which rest on the assumption that prior to beliefs must come epistemologically demonstrable supports for those beliefs, be they discovered or created.[64] Certainty is based not on the sense of *a priori* truths, and this is where there is a distinction from Kant's categories (revealed through the reflection of rational will), but based in an aspect of grammar, a belief: 'I really want to say that a language game is only possible if one trusts something (I did not say "can trust something").'[65] In believing, we submit to an authority which we can question, but not in any way that allows us to first call it into question, and then re-submit to it.[66] It is in this way that certainty requires unreflective trust; a position about which nothing is said.

> For a doubt can only exist where a question can exist, a question only where an answer exists, and an answer only where something can be said.[67]

> A person can doubt only if he has learnt certain things; as he can miscalculate only if he has learnt to calculate. In that case it is indeed involuntary.[68]

It is this level of agreement which Wittgenstein calls, in *On Certainty*, the:

> Inherited background against which I distinguish between true and false. The propositions describing this world picture might be a part of a kind of mythology. And their role is like that of rules of a game; and the game can be learned purely practically, without learning any explicit rules.[69]

This background, or mythology, is what we have to accept in order to be able to question anything at all; the formal condition of there being conditions. Thus, nothing *makes* rules correct, they are systems not of cultural hegemony but internal regularity: correctness is just what we call applying the rule; to seek an external justification is meaningless. The necessity of this quiet agreement is not based on the need for external justification, but for establishing what is right[70] through our following of rules. If, for example, we are trying to teach someone that the earth rotates around the sun[71] and they refused to accept the proof then to express doubt at this fundamental level would, says Wittgenstein, not be to question at all:

> It would be as if someone were looking for some object in a room; he opens a drawer and doesn't see it there; then he closes it again, waits, and opens it once more to see perhaps if it isn't there now, and keeps on like that. He has not learned to look for things. And in the same way this pupil has not learnt how to ask questions. He has not learnt *the* game that we are trying to teach him.[72]

The process is not wrong, it is meaningless.

Forms of life, or mythologies, however, are not envisaged by Wittgenstein as absolute. That certain beliefs are consigned to deep shadows does not mean they cannot be challenged; 'the unthought is not unthinkable'.[73] These changes can put us in the position where we can no longer proceed with the old form of life – the facts buck and we lose our seat in the saddle.[74] 'In every serious philosophical question uncertainty extends to the very roots of the problem. We must always be prepared to learn something totally new.'[75] In this way changes in what constitutes understanding, for example the switch from seeing the earth as rotating around the sun (Aristarchus)[76] to seeing the earth as a fixed body around which the sun and other planets proscribe epi-cycles (Ptolemy) and then back again to the heliocentric view (Copernicus), emerge – the notion of 'common sense' adapts, epistemologies melt and re-solidify. *Post*-relativity theory, the belief in any fixed point of rotation, may come to be seen as a bizarre piece of voodoo rather than the product of a rational outlook.[77] Wittgenstein himself talks of the 'ludicrous' suggestion that a man may ever end up on the moon as an example of orthodox certainty. Such certitude was his *inherited* background, that which he had been taught and mastered and of which his life was a unique expression. Such a background is hardened through use, yet the potential for it to revert back to a more fluid state always remains. Mythologies are under-determined because certainty, if it exists at all, is not an immutable state of affairs or being but an attitude from which we adopt a view of the world, but always *through* which we can shift to possible others.[78] Even a form of life as 'sure' in itself as mathematics requires 'a good angel'.[79] No matter how firm or 'precise' are mathematical concepts, they are inextricably linked to normative rules,[80] the requirements of which are an 'expression of an *attitude* towards a *technique* of calculating'.[81] To employ a calculating concept is to expand a series in accord with an attitude which is part of an *activity* whose propositions are true and false due to certain levels of agreement persisting throughout mathematical forms of life – the fact that, for example, mathematicians do not quarrel over the result of a calculation.[82]

These shifts are not arbitrary – they are linked to existing myths in that the new ways of looking emerge from the old language. The shift to and from the heliocentric cosmos takes place from within narrative flows such that some 'hardened' empirical propositions function as channels for the flow of those which are more fluid, but over time those which were speculative can harden, and those which were hard become fluid. Propositions can be those which are subject to tests, or those which constitute what forms a test, and these roles are never immutable.[83]

The point here is that very often we forget the possibility of things being other than they are; 'the hardness of the logical must'[84] must not seduce us into thinking it a causal, or empirical connexion between what is and what will be, between word and thing, but a grammatical connexion in which the use is already present, where the proposition is already grasped as that which defines what it is to test, prove or explain something. Things can be otherwise by virtue of these propositions slipping away. As humans our lives consist of being content to accept many things,[85] but that is not to say what these things are.

RULES AND THE PRIMITIVE

The certainty manifest in forms of life is not exhausted by cultural, or ethnological myths – the form of life is a natural – a form of *life* – as much as it is a cultural regime (anthropological can somehow capture both these senses), and it is from such primitive considerations that we can come to see how all people *can* accept these mythologies, these cultural patterns and traditions: it is a fact of our natural history that we have a deep need for conventions; that we share certain activities and physical identities; that we are charmed by certain explanations to the extent that we say 'this is how things are'.[86] The natural urge to behave regularly does not mean we are automatons, but creatures of certitude. We see the signpost and follow it with no external reference to anything else because it is part of our dynamic make-up just to do so. This is a basic fact of nature, which is distinct from a fact of natural science.

> What we are supplying are really remarks on the natural history of human beings; we are not contributing curiosities however, but observations which no one has doubted, but which have escaped remark only because they are always before our eyes.[87]

These general facts[88] are what give our lives the texture they have. The agreement manifest in the acceptance of structures as proofs, as justifications, as meaning, rests in the fact that they use words as *language*, as what we call a language, and here alone.[89] What Wittgenstein is doing is taking us back to the limits of meaningful justification, to the edge of the 'abyss',[90] to the most basic of languages:

> I want to regard man here as an animal; as a primitive being to which one grants instinct but not ratiocination. As a creature in a primitive state. Any logic good enough for a primitive means of communication needs no apology from us. Language did not emerge from some kind of ratiocination. [91]

Nor is its life an outcrop of some process of consideration;[92] what it does emerge from are intuitions or natural expressions, for example, in saying 'I have a sharp pain', where I am not describing a thing but experiencing a pain; the exclamation is a substitute which we have learnt to use instead of some pre-linguistic groan or cry: 'The origin and the primitive form of the language game is a reaction; only from this can more complicated forms develop. Language – I want to say – is a refinement, "in the beginning was the deed".'[93] We do not begin with words, but with occasions, activities,[94] gestures, facial expressions, for which words are taught. This is possible by virtue of our spontaneous species behaviour which dictates that we are able to act in accordance with the normative requirements of rules. It is only because of this that we are both able to impose regularity in terms of linguistic structures at all, and attempt to translate the languages of others using different systems of grammar. Imagine, invites Wittgenstein, a people who use coins resembling our own, in exchange for goods, but each gives what they please, and the shopkeepers hand over goods in no relation to what has been tendered. Encountering such a 'practice' reveals money to have a completely different role than ours; we feel these people as alien, much more so, suggests Wittgenstein, than 'primitives' not yet acquainted with money at all. These people may be behaving naturally, but it is beholden on us to understand the role (though the exchange may not have a specific *purpose*) of the coinage here, to know our way about, and this is possible to the extent we are able to move from our background conditions through successive reconstitutions to meld with those we have encountered. That such a practice of non-proportional exchange is so weird is suggestive of there being only a very weak sense of its being a recognizable practice, if one at all. Any translation is possible because of a natural history which acts not as a necessary end,[95] but a conditionality of expression,[96] which in no way constitutes fact. Our natural history may be primitive, but it is still contextualized in a form of life – that it has depth in no way means it *is* universal. 'The concept of a living being has the same indeterminacy as that of a language.'[97]

To explain this Wittgenstein envisages explorers encountering tribes and asks how it is possible to render their actions intelligible faithfully. The undertaking itself is only comprehensible on the assumption that there must be enough natural normative regularity between the natives' actions and their words to establish consistent connexions. Without this regularity, irrespective of any conceptual divergences based upon varying narrative traditions, there would be no language to translate. The tribes, then, can be strange, but they are not alien, in the way that spherical Martians with sticks coming out of their sides,[98] or even the coiners mentioned previously, would be alien. It is possible to imagine norms other than our own, other myths, other conditions of expression and with such stories show how movement becomes possible, for we know what to look for – natural facts like facial expressions, gestures and so on. Take, for example, the builders and their language game introduced at the start of *Philosophical Investigations*. The builders appear silent, isolate, almost dull occupiers of a stark mono-dimension, people of whom it can be said, by us, that they hardly take an interest in the world. Despite this their activity is certainly identifiable as at least occupying the threshold of, or is suggestive of, a primitive sense of imagination, understanding, sense and so on.[99] The tribes encountered by the explorer need not be of such a weird and displaced hue. Tribal rhythms are far more complex than those of the builders, their myths are less enclosed and their norms less annulling; but for the explorer to understand the pulse of this rhythmic activity there must be a sense of continuity; an intelligible way in which connexions between the explorer and the tribe can be made. So 'The common behaviour of mankind is the system of reference by means of which we interpret an unknown language'[100] but such behaviour is not determinate in itself. Wittgenstein reiterates this point when he asks us to consider 'under what circumstances will the explorer say: The word ". . ." of this tribe means the same as our "and so on"?' with reference to their showing what a rule means. It is the circumstances, 'the details of their life and their language' which justify him in so translating from one instance to another.[101] The explorer is able to so interpret because he occupies a world with language, as do the tribe, and it is this shared assimilation with regularity which renders possible feelings of understanding. Translation involves an appreciation of the role played by specific words in specific language games (their connexions, positions, etc.) from which emerges an understanding of a localized constancy of use. This is manifest in our working towards the tribe – gradually imagining moves which take us from our language games to theirs.[102]

We can understand other forms of life; they are not hermetically sealed off from each other, the boundaries are blurred and cross-over points allow a foothold to 'outsiders' who remain 'insiders' in the sense that they inhabit a world with language.[103] The other may seem queer to us, even to the extent that incommensurability between concepts may arise, but this does not imply that others do not have other concepts which criss-cross our own to the extent that essentially different concepts are always imaginable, that the recognition of normative regularity in the behaviour of others does not require a life which runs in the same direction as those others,[104] and that what is certain is that there will always be others who are uncertain.[105]

Language is dependent upon an environment of use.[106] Such an environment is never universal but possesses 'rough edges'[107]which shift, and in doing so occasionally rub up against us. This abrasive relationship with myth is coupled with the more continual and usual one of immersion. In such relations repulsion and seduction work in tandem; there is no single force, only criterial equilibria, such that: 'If in life we are surrounded by death, so too in the health of our intellect we are surrounded by madness.'[108] Conceptions of what it is to be a human self with an identity are of a kaleidoscopic hue. The condition is an occupation of what are a multiplicity of constituted systems constantly open to reconstitution. In being content to accept many things there is no definitive list of what it is we must accept – just that acceptance at some level is a necessary aspect of who we are.

This leaves human rights in a curious position. Forbidden on pain of unintelligibility to grope for a conception of a transcendental self on which to orientate themselves, and cast as rules which are followed as aspects of myths or forms of life, human rights as grammatical rules are very much aspects of ordinary language use. To be made sense of, the only way they can be spoken of is as those rules which act as criteria for the form of life that is the human species itself. Whilst subject to change, as all forms are, this would at least make plausible any claim that to respect human rights is somehow to acknowledge what it is to be a language user and all that this entails: the recognition of the difference between things; the acceptance of authority as belief and trust; the eschewal of immutables; and so on. In articulating such criteria human rights need to embrace the flux and mutability of the human condition, without thereby collapsing any sense of what they are conditions of, the human species, into an entirely random and accidental chance conflation of events. This requires an analysis of just what sense can be given to the idea of human being as language user, one conceived as a linguistic self.

3 Linguistic selves

We take our fetters with us; our freedom is not total: we still turn
our gaze towards the things we have left behind; our imagination
is full of them.

(Montaigne 'On Solitude' in *The Complete Essays*, trans.
M. A. Screech, Penguin, 1996, p. 269)

The political resonance of Wittgenstein's work on language is never
immediate, apparent or ideologically strident, but the emerging ideas
of self and identity portend necessary shifts in political perspective
towards the convoluted and contingent common spaces of the everyday, most notably within the foundationally inspired fields of neo-
Kantian and Cartesian rights discourse. What is of import here are
the conditions, criteria or significations of being a linguistic self. If
private language is chimerical, and behaviourism its structural
adjunct, then what stands in the stead of the progenitors, these
spaces of the first cause, creativity and contemplation? To understand
criteria requires investigation in narrative perspicuity and use. Rather
than look to foundations an investigation focuses upon instances,
enunciations, speech acts, a focus which radicalizes by virtue of its
invoking an internal, grammatical connexion between self and identity as opposed to proffering rival substantive cores to the self.
Being conceived grammatically the self is a force of resonance, or
creative appropriateness, a force which can be acknowledged, har-
nessed, shown, challenged but which cannot be proved, justified or
known about in terms of finally fixed co-ordinates.

Cartesian doubt and Kantian duty attempted to expunge the perpetual possibility of otherness, of accident, of chance and of temporality from relations of understanding. Surety lay somewhere; a
residence called mind, or category, camouflaged by obscurantist practices and procedures, by the ignorance of the myopic and by the

drabness of the eternally content. Human rights discourse has occupied such a residence; as human beings our goal is to realize those conditions to which we can utterly and absolutely prostrate ourselves, in order that we become what we are by ourselves, for ourselves. These conditions of passivity ensure all begin from the beginning, understood as beings of equal worth capable of autonomous action we are to go forth and do. But in taking up what is other from within ordinary language there emerges in the guise of rival, priest, peer, disciple, muse, sibling or lover such identities to *be made or created*. What is other than ourselves, what faces us, occupies our own identity, is the facing – an internal and immanent relation with the foreign. If self and identity are not givens but shift as possible creations signified by imagination and baptized by language games[1] then it seems it is the criteria by which these instances or moments reach moments of equilibrium or absorption or destruction that require investigation.

Ontologically – though anti-transcendentalist Wittgenstein is never a constructivist relying upon the fickle manoeuvrings of a fetid as well as florid eternal deferral which leaves us prey to the vicissitudes of relativism and performative contradiction (using reason to violate rational rules) – language games, forms of life and basic facts show that self and identity rest with a regularity in use made grammatically apparent. Ours is not a relation of knowing to the world, we do not approach the world as a representation *and then interpret it*, for this presupposes the now defunct disembodied will elicited in Tractatan transcendentalism; to see something is not reducible to its becoming materialized within us where the within refers to an immutable place from which the other is not a facing, but hazy and ragged impressions cast by a misdirected squint.[2] The will reacts to things continuously – it is, as Nietzsche sees it, a grammatical fiction, not a causing entity: we have an attitude to the world, a place from which we see the world *as something*. The self becomes something like a collection of possible perspectives – it partakes of the many myths which hold us, it expresses something as felt[3] existence, it is the companion of the world; a world which no longer waxes and wanes as a whole but dawns and dissolves in accordance with learnt imaginations. But actually what this we, or self, or will is here remains problematic and in need of exploration. Problematic because whilst it cannot replace the noumena as a rival theoretical construction, it must have some force as an entity (grammatical) for it to work as a tether for instances of ordinary human rights use. Exploration rather than justification because without such a journey of vision, of seeing things from various perspectives, the problematic risks becoming a hidden confusion.

THE LINGUISTIC SELF AS PUPIL OF RULES AND MYTH

As language users human selves are taught to follow rules, and this increasing familiarization breeds adeptness – our judgements become more and more refined,[4] our activities are consummated in language – in our language games rests an entire culture of which we it seems are a holographic embodiment. But this pupilage is not just an indoctrination in the runes of folklore, it is also an invitation to take up from where the teacher leaves off. To master techniques, to inhabit inherited mythologies, to see things from this aspect and now that aspect, to engage in practices like calculating, arguing, painting and loving, is not just to exhibit a specific type of isolate behaviour, but to act in ways which have a place in our on-going lives (we do not just argue or interpret but argue with someone to persuade them of the validity of a specific case, or see something as something and not something else). Such a mastery of learning takes place in the regimes of living themselves – the established spaces of identity which exist neither as revelatory realizations of invariant essence nor as enclosed and conditioned reflexive responses, but as limits inviting both occupation and deviation. In learning we are not imitating *per se* but understanding that *this* or *that* is the point at which the spade turns; in this instance this is where we confirm our inheritance, our myth. It may be we encounter a weird, a distressing, a charming or a repulsive context in which the spade turning makes less sense; where what we learn is brought into sharp relief. Imagine a child instructed in conventions of non-violence and compassion entering an abattoir; or the suprematist painter Kasimir Malevich providing as an instance of painting nothing but a white square; or a maths student encountering non-linear functions; or being embroiled in the turmoil of unrequited love. We can use established practices to resolve these antinomies but only by warping them, by invoking the rules in particular ways. In absorbing rules we are making them our own; we are using them in contexts which cannot be predicted. This is what is all too human.

So the mastery of rules is not akin to some form of divine supplication where initiates populate every nook and cranny of an ultimate blueprint; where, unable to conceive of deviation, they ossify under the weight of endlessly repeated ritual. If such was the case then living would be as silted up and as leaden with procedure as the

fictional world view of Mervyn Peake's *Gormenghast* where resistance
is indistinguishable from nonsense. But even in Peake's world idio-
syncracies of character emerge; challenge creeps from the cracks in
the stone-clad lineage of the ancient language games. It is less a
world of closure than one alluding to potential gaps in spaces and
places, and can be read less as fantasy than as its reproof – the
character Steerpike is the human revealed; through him the continuous seeing from just one perspective or aspect is disrupted. Though
sodden with ritual there is still scope for change; motion and disruption run in tandem with fidelity and habit.

Likewise, and more pressingly, there is the totalizing aspiration of
the practice of torture. In its belittling of self, its purpose of degrada-
tion, it requires complete submission. But this can never be absolute.
In appropriating the pain and insistence of the regime the victim is
humiliated in the face of that gravest and most rotten of images –
oneself, but such forms are never complete. The victim can survive
and go beyond the realization of their own mortality and depravity,
and not merely through outright defiance and the preservation of an
aloof conviction. They occupy relations which extend outside of the
torture chamber to friends, struggles and aims that do not belong as
possessions to the victim (and hence cannot be taken away), nor
which can be reduced to theory or knowledge, but which imbue
their perspectives – they may well be rot, but they are not just rot.[5]
Conditions, even the poorest, are textured and the forms occasioned
by them and occasioning of them are not so flat and smooth as to
offer no grip. Forms occupy and are occupied by numerous facings;
alternatives, tangents and potentials as much as established facias,
and it is the concomitant possibility of things being other than they
are which makes individuation intelligible and totalizing unintelligible. We need not know these possible facings but must be aware
of their possibility.

Without the idea of this facing a culture becomes static, exhausted,
a husk in which language itself would have no ambience. In following
rules grammatical selves are less preserving an edifice than imaginatively exploring their inexactitude from within an atmosphere of
common understandings – language games resemble temporarily
insulated imperfections; regular behaviour which can be eroded,
warped and toyed with as much as confirmed. As Cavell says, there
is a sense in which learning language involves not only repeated
attempts at getting it right but *taking over* from where the teacher
leaves off – 'Ah!, now *I* can go on'. The pupil can see language as
an inheritance to be wrestled away from the teacher and re-applied

in new contexts.[6] To absorb completely the teachings is to envisage the possibility of moving to a new field of being we imaginatively create from established rules of grammar. The pupil becomes exponent, capable of variation, individuation and disruptive gesture – 'handing on is handing over'.[7] Learning is as much about the dissolution and violence made possible by an increasing familiarity with a world with language, as it is about continued conformity with that world – there are no privileged positions, including that of language and we are talking about a world of undetermined possibilities, not of essences.[8] The presence of the linguistic self is what breathes life into signs; its alterity, iteration and enjoining ensures that language is a building and eroding force; it can at times eat away at itself, for words only have use in so far as they resonate with the taught and appropriating capacities of imagination, appreciation and creativity.

In such a mêlée self and identity cannot be asserted as conforming to an absolute transcendental state, the subjectivity of originating unity is moribund, but nor can it be confined to a will-o'-the-wisp character flitting between whim, preference and potentially useful experience. The whole thrust of the Wittgensteinian lesson is to erode dualisms inherent in asserting generalized conditions such as true/false, universal/particular, public/private. Self and identity are framed in a *world of experience* which is not reducible to a world of knowledge or truth, be it structural or solipsistic. The self is a connective force which is never absolutely constituted nor constituting but a being who has learnt and is learning the uses of language in infinitely possible contextual ways. The identity of this self is found in those aspects it takes up and grasps as defining or representational, aspects which exist at narrative distances of grammatical non-contradiction, distances established by temporary cessations (which can still, however, last a lifetime) in the habitation and exploration of the limits of language. These aspects are brought about by disruption as much as discussion (pragmatically useful) or discovery (principle), and once used become norms internally linked with the motive force of agency and the power of articulation – norms concerning what it makes *sense* to say and which we come to accept as providing the criteria by which what we come to say is said to be intelligible.

Clearly these norms or codes of recognition and acknowledgement are contingent upon there being certain forms of life within which certain types of regularity (not truth) are established. We are all of us mythologized. The linguistic self and identity exist in fields of grammar. But this need not be a perpetual internment; indeed the very problematic Wittgenstein describes is our tendency to view the world ideologically, as myth *save for* the single instance of true identity of self, which in our Western case, the bourgeois, scientist view, is the inviolable core being. Likewise, to escape from internment does not rely upon the necessity of violence, of replacing one hegemonic myth with a perpetual anti-essentialist an-other, for the alteric hue to language games reveals a relational as opposed to merely intentional motion in regularity. The self is focused through the mutuality of language games; identity as an aspect of self is wrought not merely as a resistance to the systemic force of tradition, convention and orthodox rules, but in their active use. Identity is not predicated on nomadic hostility alone. Deleuze and Guattari's nomad is a wanderer beyond the pale, it evokes that aspect of the self which perpetually encounters the dawning of aspects, which moves amongst the smooth space of new possibilities, but which only make sense by virtue of an understanding which has been fully passed on in a continuing relation with the existing world of language. Aspect dawning arises from the grasping of and a continuation of the myth.

The nomadic bent of the linguistic self is akin to what de Certeau calls a tactician. The self, though they occupy established representations or disciplinary mechanisms or regimes or systems which act as regulatory fields, is able to outwit them using tactical tropes of trickery, illusion, cunning, manipulation, aggression, hope and the exploration of marginality. The strategy postulates a place of established power relations, a fixed abode of appropriated, possessed rules which render the necessary knowledge for the constitution and maintenance of this space in the face of delineated exteriors, what is outside. The tactician eschews such space, operating devoid of formal locus they grasp foreign rules, but imperfectly, and in doing so meld and disrupt them. They look to opportunity, they poach what is the other.[9] The tactician exploits possibilities consequent upon an infiltration of circumstances, they manipulate the spaces created by the established strategic forces with ruse and guile.[10]

So the linguistic self is both tactician and strategist, a centripetal force holding together aspectival identities linked through family resemblance and embroiled in the real, fragmented circumstances of ordinary living. There is no purified, isolate unity of bleached being beyond such a kaleidoscopic and often murky world. There is a continual movement between iteration, effraction and creation whereby in repeating the myth in use there arises the possibility of, at certain moments, dissolution. In the complete absorption of certain aspects the self exhausts the instances of the lessons and goes on to encounter the lessons as lessons, and thence the dawning of others. Thus as well as being iterative, a vessel of taught lessons, a strategist, the linguistic self is also effractive – as it repeats it dissolves, it explores, it poaches, it bends, it uses tactics and in so doing is creative – it comes to occupy (and hence use as definitions or representations) other places, or strategies or games. In grasping commonly felt satisfactions and dissatisfactions whose resonance is less logically compelling than inherited, taught or adopted styles of being with substantive value,[11] the linguistic self employs tactics as styles of disruption, insinuation and aesthetic use. In doing so it is acting – the re-negotiation, re-description, re-assessment and re-assertion of established strategies, striated spaces or myths.

So mythologies, states of continual seeing, are not equivalent to great slabs of wax in which we are forever set, nor to continental plates which drift with glacial fatigue; institutional tectonics or strategies are inherently incomplete. Whilst identity and self are nothing without context, this context is less than totalizing – moments of crisis, destruction and manipulation in the fields of identity are possible; our relation of continual seeing becomes congested, collapsing under the disorderly presence of what is beyond that which has been fully understood: this mien of otherness, a presence of new dawns and new ways, is what is beyond the condition of established possibility;[12] a forage into new dimensions which forces change in identities; we see the world anew – yet in a related sense, still being beholden upon the lessons of old as ladders which once climbed are kicked aside, but not away. The constancy of incompleteness requires the linguistic self to be aware of what is other as a facing, the beyond as deponent – something passive in form but active in possible or imaginative sense, which may well become proponent or interlocutor in some indeterminate future space.

THE LINGUISTIC SELF, IMAGINATION AND WILL

To see new aspects, to experience aspect dawning, demands an imagination[13] to see an image first one way, then another. To see aspects is to exercise will,[14] a capacity for style which erodes the curvature and corporeality of strategic systems or regimes by isolating the plasticity of relations between tactical and strategic selves, evoking a sense in which selves are selves in some way distinct from specific representations of the world but still immersed in the relations of grammar.[15] So whilst aspects have a specific feel, ring, resonance and tone because of an involvement with language which begins with basic repetition, imitation, reward and so on, they also require an imagination, will and style which can be so acute that they shift; they move beyond by exhausting current possibilities.

Will is imaginative in that it gives vent to being in an intelligible world. To have strategy and tactics is to occupy background conditions of certainty by ways of enunciation, action, approach which are contextually rooted. The will is an active and complex feeling of command and execution made by the arrest in the babble of emotions with which we are beset as language users.[16] The will is expressed through the specific metabolisms of the various myths of which it partakes – to have will is to be caught up and taken along by established tempos, rhythms and harmonies of established forms – but on such a musical travelogue phenomena are not of the real world; our will is not met by the limits of a separate reality, they are both caught up in imagination. Thus to have will is both to command and to obey, it denotes a grammatical sense of self (as opposed to a possessive or absolutely sovereign subject) whereby to will is to occupy established regimes of constraint, compulsion, motion and to use these forces of resistance to overcome them. We can conceive of the idea of will only by virtue of our being immersed in the techniques of language games imaginatively conceived. Thus willing is 'complicated', less a unity, a denoted subject, than an amalgam of aversions, attractions and metabolisms whereby the self moves beyond constraints by virtue of a disturbed, or powerful, occupation of those constraints.[17]

Thus immersion in language games provokes imaginative responses; only when we have a firm grasp and sensitive nose[18] for the imponderable evidence, the subtleties of glance, the gestures, the tone or hint, which we recognize but find ourselves unable to describe, can we witness the dawning of new aspects, the urge to go beyond. Mulhall suggests this gestural familiarity transcribes the limits of the language game. We have moved in understanding from tool acquisition through mastery to aesthetic gesture; from the purely mimetic to the truly creative and once turgid, replete, we are able to carry the gesture, the imponderable over itself, to a new language game distinct from, though historically and narratively beholden to, the existing one.[19] Herein lies the autobiographical moment, the movement from a world found to a world suggested; self-construction appropriate for and sensitive to the narrative or contextual environment from which it issues. Integral to such a creative act is the presence of language as gesture, ritual, found in the motion not of words but the presence of a human face.

In following a rule a self has to partake and exemplify this imponderable evidence – tone, gesture, hint. Language is not confined to the issuing of mere words, sentences, commands and the like but extends to encompass the subtlest of movements, the vaguest of hints and ranges from the inchoate to the explicit. It is the very over-determinancy of linguistic identity, whose only completeness is found in the state of self-subjectifying absorption of explored linguistic limits which heralds the potential embrace of new identities, that ensures rule following cannot be undertaken by anything other than humans: the imaginative embodiment of grammatical rules distinguishes the human forms of life from those of the animal kingdom or even learning machines. To use language is an aesthetic, imaginative engagement with the imponderable, it is not mimetism. So it is that if a lion could speak we would not understand. But what of machines – if they can be said to follow rules, be taught to learn from mistakes, to follow patterns of logical reason, to appreciate the minutiae of context, and by *humans* – then why is it only humans who follow grammatical rules, and not their metallic siblings? In resisting the conflation of the mechanical impulse with the grammatical Wittgenstein was able to reveal not just the crucial influence of imponderable evidence, but the primal force of the face in linguistic relations.

THE SELF AND MACHINES

When we teach or are taught rules we expect or display a specific reaction to instruction; this reaction of regularity, 'which is our guarantee of understanding, presupposes as a surrounding particular circumstances, particular forms of life and speech. (As there is no such thing as a facial expression without a face.) (This is an important movement of thought.)'[20] It is this movement, this recognition of 'just how much there is to the physiognomy in what we call "following a rule" in everyday life'[21] that shows why it is machines cannot be said to follow rules *in the grammatically relevant way*, and hence why rule following strategies and the tactics of linguistic selves follow a specifically human locus. They are inextricably woven with the imponderable evidence. Crucially, if machines came to have a face *à la* Philip Dick's replicants in *Do Androids Dream of Electric Sheep?*, beings who could only be distinguished from humans by an investigation of the nuanced dilations of the pupil in response to emotive questioning, then these boundaries could perhaps be appropriated by beings other than humans. The point is not that machines are never going to be able have a face, but that possessing them requires their being something other than machines.

Artificial intelligence is understood as an algorithmic, electronic life force manifest in 'thinking' machines. If thought is conceived of linguistically and language is characterized by rule following then what, so the reasoning goes, other than paranoid perfectionism, is to prevent machines entering the realm of the conscious? Machines, wired up with commands they have been 'taught' receive information which they process and to which they respond, just as the senses transfer data to language users via neuronal synapse and processing units which then issue responses manifest in muscular action or utterance via phonemes. As discrete logical systems there is little to tell between rule following humans and machines; only outward appearance renders them distinct. If thought is the product of an inner complex of rules, the expression of an inner identity manifest in a process, then it equates very well with the computational procedures of machines.

The most forceful and eloquent investigation of these possibilities comes in Alan Turing's work on computable numbers which formed the nascent conjectures of the now burgeoning science of artificial intelligence.[22] In *Computing, Machinery and Intelligence*[23] he created the 'imitation game', a process designed to supplant the question 'Can machines think?' In this game an unsighted interrogator, via an interpreter whose presence enabled the response to be differentiated from whom (what?) was giving it, must distinguish between a machine imitating a human and a human, both of whom (which?) are answering her questions. If she cannot tell the difference between the outputs then thinking can be attributed to the machine. Envisage a variation on a chess game where a player is in combat with both a machine and another human, each initiating moves. The opponents remain unsighted from each other, and the objective of the game is for the single player to tell the other two apart by analysing the moves made by each.

Turing had envisaged that a machine could mimic a human through the translation of observed human behaviour into an instruction table, a set of rules, which would subsequently govern the finite and definite configurations of the machine. As the machine engaged in the imitation game it would learn through logical inference and probability. The machine could be programmed to act according to learnt imperatives which governed the order of rule application, such that, for example, if one method of action proves quicker than another, though they both yield the same result, then the quicker one is to be given preference.[24] Thus, as Turing envisaged, instructions could be produced by the machine itself through a kind of scientific induction.

Stuart Shanker[25] points out that Turing never bestows cognitive ability upon machines; machine thought is only manifest in what he terms the shift from 'brute facts' to 'learning programmes', the instructions contained within the latter being dependent upon some non-cognitive expressions of the former such as the working through of algorithmic procedure. The categorical leap from brute facts to self-modifying algorithms is not one of overt cognition but of the capacity to learn and improve upon previous performance. The machine is able to alter its own rules, rules which consist of algorithms, sub-rules devoid of cognitive content which determine the 'state of mind' of the machine. What Turing is trying to show is that although the machine is necessarily defined by algorithms, fragmented human rules of calculation and spatial awareness, rules whose meaning the machine cannot actually know, the machine can still be said to be thinking because the essence of thought 'is a function of the complexity of the programme which the computer [the machine] follows rather than the individual steps of the algorithm'.[26] Despite the fact that a machine which uses algorithms cannot comprehend the meaning of the rules which the algorithms go to make up, it can still think because its output, the result of any number of finite manipulations, remains indistinguishable from that of any human. In calculating a sum of numbers it is a 'computer'.

Just as two chimps can be said to follow a rule within a context of mistakes, teaching, practising, etc., so it is with calculation. Rule following is internally related to regularity but it cannot be reduced to it; learning extends beyond simple (reducible) regularity and repetition and towards treating rules as making space for invitations, moments of openness. Calculation is a publicly defeasible process. For a human to be able to employ a rule, even an algorithm, is to do more than merely mimic the successive avoidance of error or the following of certain progressions; it involves an ability to show, using a background of established semantic and syntactic techniques and purposes, just what is the case in this situation.[27] To follow a rule is not just to reveal existing, pre-programmed connexions or instances of regularity (as, say, natural science avows, though not necessarily practices[28]) but to create certain connexions by emphasizing certain aspects rather than others: 'To claim that "x" is the same action as "y" can be to make a connexion between them rather than simply to record a pre-existing relationship.'[29] To follow rules also requires an imaginative capacity to realize the potential for possible re-deployment, subversion, tangential reasoning and the like. This imagination is best captured in the physiognomy of being, the body language, the imponderable evidence of ordinary language and in asking the person to play against unknown opponents the imitation game fails to acknowledge this.

Just as such a machine cannot fully follow a rule of language so a language user cannot use a meaningless rule. To posit the reducing of recursive functions to sets of mechanically calculable units so as to make it possible that by performing the totality of these tasks the machine would perform the function Turing had to invoke the idea of sub-rules or algorithms. He was wrong to assume, however, that algorithms, no matter how simple or regular, reduce complexity; they are just another set of rules applicable because of a different context which, says Shanker, reflects the fact that different rules in different contexts display differing degrees of efficacy. The decomposition of rules does not dissolve their normative content, and normative action cannot be represented by a causal nexus of mental events which the language user somehow discovers inside of themselves, so to speak, nor can these norms be encoded, for they extend into the imaginative. For Turing the human condition, in true reductive fashion, is broken into parts, such that the whole becomes an agglomeration of external results (neurone firings, psychological predilections, secretions of the hypothalamus and so on). What this explanation ignores is that understanding and creativity are not single performances, they partake of historical and narrative conditions of expression, and these criteria are not programmes or processes but conditions of what it is to be a rule follower. They are part of and not peripheral to rule following for they permit the possibility of our having *an attitude* towards others that encompasses their being rule followers.[30]

It is then through imaginative relations with aspects that the grammatical self forms as the shifting equilibrium brought about by identities linked through historically and narratively cast family resemblances. The self, its identities and the facing exist as total aspects of each other related in the continual grasping of circumstance; they are riven with a perpetual awareness of the possible distinctions, variations and multiplicities[31] inherent in the fullest expression of language games whose meanings are cast as ritual,

custom, ceremony, movement. This is well expressed as an anthropological state of being for the self, which acknowledges the importance
of regularity, stage setting and established theme and tradition to the
establishing of aspectival identities whilst still retaining an appreciation and wariness of the incompleteness of such strategies and
regimes given the possible emergence of the facing, the other that
faces us when acting as tactician. To understand identity anthropo-
logically is to see it as a collection of enunciations tethered in contextual systems of grammar. To enunciate is to articulate actively, to
situate the speech act in a relation with an other (the facing), to
appropriate the rules of language and finally to specify a now.[32]
In so acting, speaking from somewhere, translating between some-
wheres, the meanings of words are never completely arrested but
shift amongst dispersed myths, conjunctions, strategies and forms of
life. They take established, organized and managed spaces, and, in
so appropriating, incur the possibility of shifts in spatial forms
through the use of displacement, alliteration, metaphor, repressions,
accidents and so on. Anthropology encompasses both the managed
totems and possible effractive relations consequent upon their continuing use in everyday practices.

The linguistic self and anthropological identities make redundant
the question of just where meaning *resides* (self, community, environment, universe or nowhere) and make prominent the question of
where it *arises*, in what contexts aspect seeing (as doing) takes place.
The idea is to make enigmatic the character of life and its many
aspects (novel, alluring, boring, depraving, illusory, distorting, en-
nobling, etc.), not to clear up the enigma of living by reducing it to
a state of knowledge, be it intelligible, rational, sexual, biological or
whatever. The purity of logical form is alluring, but an empty and
misleading requirement if generalized because it gives us no grip, friction – we are dealing with an ideal, an abstraction, and not with
living: 'We want to walk: so we need *friction*. Back to the rough
ground!'[33] But this rough ground is less than philosophically comfortable; we ache for the annihilation of doubt and confusion; we
lust for tranquillity – this is our tragedy and of this we should be
ever wary; horizons of the ultimate, including the ultimately confined,
are but false dawns. How we are to resist the allure of their specious
glow is by developing a sensitivity to the myths beyond our own, by
using an anthropological nose, by acknowledging the possibility of
what is other than ourselves.

THE SELF AND MYTHS

In his remarks upon the anthropologist J.G. Frazer's *Golden Bough* Wittgenstein is insistent that the sensitivity he encourages to other ways of life, one which Frazer singularly lacks, is not a legitimization of the often weird (animal sacrifice for the absolution of guilt; the placing of stones in trees to slow down a setting sun) but an exhortation to become aware of how it is cultural practices often hold us captive. It is not just the 'crude' magic of the tribal peoples which is so entrancing, but all myths, including science and universalist metaphysics; and it is the latter, being more sophisticated and powerful in terms of empirical control than their traditional tribal counterparts, that are all the more dangerous[34] – their generality suffocates the necessary distinctions between things. Wittgenstein is not hostile to myth; we all invoke ritual, it renders our lives more comfortable and capable, so long as we do not get too myopic and invoke myth beyond myth.

Being steeped in the scientist form of life Frazer, like many observers and explainers, was accustomed to view things causally – to see actions, traditions, customs and narratives as predicated on some form of means–end reasoning. Though plausible, 'the insidious thing about the causal point of view is that it leads us to say "Of course it has to happen like that." Whereas we ought to think: it may have happened like that – and also in many other ways.'[35] This is how science can send us to sleep and deny us the humility of wonder,[36] fettered as we are by the 'mind forg'd manacles' that are the dark and satanic Baconian natural laws. Why did the tribe kill the chicken in a ritual gathering or outside the kitchens or in the market place – to know rests on a locality.[37] To effect a form of causal explanation in each case is to hanker after the linear links of progressive or regressive functions by which science so often proffers explanation. But the observation of cause and effect assumes we are dealing with specific states of knowledge here – Frazer sees the tribe as aspiring scientists, potential controllers of the external environment, when the ritual killing may well not be an issue of control at all. Knowledge persists by virtue of criteria which can be as much an acknowledgement of limits as aspirations for predictive power. It may be a form of prayer, an acknowledgement of limits, and this we will only come to understand once we are aware of the role such ritual plays in their form of life as a whole. We have to understand what Rhees calls the 'spirit' internal to the gesture of ritual; observation and the importation of assumption is not sufficient.[38]

In viewing ways of life and the identities embodying them anthro-
pologically Wittgenstein is not asking us to ask how can a people
possibly believe in such practices, but how *do* they believe. Science
can look to the efficacious results; it explains, but only in part. In
Freud's words Frazer's examinations of primitive totemic rituals
cannot escape arbitrary preference, being 'too rational to take into
consideration the effective character of what they explain'.[39] The
depth, disquiet and diurnal nature of ritualistic killings seem to flow
along a different river bed from that of rationalistic control. To
understand other forms of life we need to build bridges not over
rivers but between them, and this is achieved from a sensitivity to
continuums. Freud, for example, believed totemistic practices to be
as prevalent amongst the sophisticates as the primitives, linking it
with Oedipal complex and castration complex experienced in a
father–son rivalry for the sexual affections of the mother. By dis-
placing the unconscious frustrations and hate, mingled with a history
of affection for the father for having succoured the child, upon a
totemistic icon such as an animal for whom a total identification
and highly ambivalent affections were displayed, people were no less
mythologized.[40] Using inventive perspectives Freud melds one form
of life with another through strange and alluring bonds – likening
the emergence of ritual, gesture, myth and totem to a psychic reality
whose ambivalences are as rife in modern as in primitive conditions.
Freud reveals the hostility felt towards the primal father, which in
primitive societies is fully and immediately acknowledged in the full
fact of deed, as hidden behind the inhibited ceremony of the
neurotic.[41] Instead of attempting to correct the savage Freud urges
the observer to follow the instance of deed more closely, to examine
the prototype of the neurosis itself, thereby seeking connectives
using racial psychology.

Very often, then, our observations and explanations are not based
on evidence at all, even when we are being 'scientific', but on speculation. We are inclined or disinclined to accept things as a repetition of
what has gone on before – as is the case with Wittgenstein's investigation of Freud's analysis of dreams, wish fulfilment and obsession.[42]
Freud provides us with a brilliantly conceived new mythology –
turgid with the imponderable evidence of the conscious he slipped
into the unconscious thereby opening a new realm of being. But the
fact we are inclined to think that an event, for instance, the obses-
sional behaviour exhibited by Freud's 'Rat Man' case of 1909, is a
constellation of dispositions (paranoia, forgetfulness, cowardice)
explained by accidental motions of fate (the conjunction of a story

on rat torture, an unpaid gambling debt, broken spectacles), need not collapse into a general law of science. Freud's speculations were valuable as alternative interpretations of what we experience – dreams become symbols which render an explicative context such that their appearance is explained by the conjunction of unconscious reflection on repressed childhood urges coupled with an analyst's hypothesis based on previous cases. But Freud was not proving laws here – things were not always this way – not *every* dream is possessed of the essence of sexually orientated wish fulfilment; rather he is creating a new myth; an alluring way of seeing things.[43] Exploring the peripheries of the unconscious with such a vibrant display of irreverence for the neuroses of modern, bourgeois living was to be respected, but to collapse it into a generalizing science was to emasculate its perspicuity, was to recapture it for the stable purposes of orthodoxy.

Just as is the case with looking at other tribes, we can speculate valuably, we can adopt a point of view; but why reduce this to questions of generalized right and wrong? There is no right interpretation at all – there is no universal reason why people dream, or kill, as they do; there are many each of which partakes in myth. The idea of establishing more correct symbols for things is not an option here; we do not need to invent an alternative paradigm but work within, through and thence beyond existing strategies by looking tactically at the different methods of representation or symbolization used in ordinary language. Different grammatical conventions are appropriate for different ways of making sense.

So myths never swamp the self – we can create new concepts, speculate along tangential trajectories using the tools of myth as did Freud, perhaps even move beyond the myth in a blaze of post-analytic Foucauldian aspiration for truth speaking (*parrhesia*), but in doing so we are not encountering or moving towards the absolute myth. What we are doing is affective as well as cognitive, we are aestheticizing existence, evoking an art of being, of creating a self and identity from within the established grammatical lines of forms of life. These aesthetic movements of seeing aspects are open to us all – only most of us desist from the effort, being embroiled in the certitude of non-creative repetition, or the more irksome process of active resistance to the tide of generalities which Wittgenstein found so suffocating.

THE SELF AND TRUTH

The self is wrought in the centripetal force of anthropological identities whose aspects range from imitation through reflective and active effraction to possible aesthetic transformative states where the self and facing meld. This furnace is not the home of Vulcan or some other god but the ordinary language user who is faced with the imaginative task of seeing aspects. The obvious critique of ordinary language philosophy, especially when used politically, is that not only does it jeopardize the rigorous pursuit of truth or the ideal, it also confines us to a mutilated condition of modernist vacuity with no appreciation of the structural and ideological forces working to promote such reflective myopia.[44] In encouraging us to look for identities which are already there Wittgenstein is pushing us into the straitjacket of paranoia, 'a cosy and self-justifying cocoon of conceptual custom'[45] in which the enemy is the alien, the untried, the parasite, the dreamer. But of course Wittgenstein is not asserting what is right or wrong, true or false, here. The spade turns for the self – its identity is simply what it does; to say there is an end to explanation and justification here is to blast aside the cosy and coy world of certainty and embrace the tragic one where myth is never complete, where everydayness can be, though need not be, weird as much as it is normal, where seriousness blends with comic, where the zealous feed off the weak and slackers create culture.[46] The myth grips us only to drop us and pick us up again someplace else. The truth is a combination of systems of representation and will which is understood when pupils of their own accord passionately take up the positions on the crennelation of strategic places in some sort of calm and mutual seizure;[47] but through such a seizure the self conceives of what is beyond and begins to make manoeuvres in its direction, and the more it shifts, the more it acknowledges itself through gesture, the greater is the sense of challenge and disquiet in light of encroaching otherness. There is nothing like *the truth* out there:

> No one can speak of the truth; if he has not mastered himself. He cannot speak it; – but not because he is not yet clever enough. The truth can be spoken only by someone who is already at home in it; not by someone who still lives in falsehood and reaches out from falsehood towards truth on just one occasion.[48]

Grammatical truth does not abandon the possibility of criticism; the self eschews reasons and invokes the tactic of persuasion, of demonstration – 'this is how it is' and not the nonsensical 'this is how it

must be'. Relativism is only an issue on pain of a performative contradiction where truth is something scattered equally amongst specific
practices, or Kuhnian paradigms, seen from a position of totality,
which is exactly the position the assertion seeks to avoid. As a question it seeks to transcend what we do in order to assess what we do,
and so is no question at all.[49] Wittgenstein is describing how truth is
used in accordance with criteria which are accepted, absorbed, inherited not by virtue of the self being satisfied with its correctness but
because they partake of a form of life. Truth is always under a grammatical description[50] – created through sanction, technique, mastery,
status, and is intimately connected to the locality of purpose. It is
much like a technique of suasive force with one self speaking for
another, or themselves, in terms of the appropriateness of specific
identities. It cannot be asserted definitively, but authoritatively given
as a *felt* commitment of a self at a narrative distance of grammatical
non-contradiction.

THE SELF AND CORE BEING

The convention of human rights ascription, given that what delineates as human is the face, the gesture, the learning, the grammar
and not the reason, the control or absolute reality, rests upon certain
norms referring to their coherent employment; for example to children and not to deckchairs, thistles or wind-up toy mice, and to all
humans, not just a selective bunch. What counts as sensible use is
taught and accepted by linguistic selves immersed in specific grammatical structures – we measure, assess and value in accordance with
convention and not with what is true or false. As such, to say
machines have human rights is not a contradiction, for this implies
conditions could arise where the contradiction could be resolved,
but nonsensical given our existing rules of grammar.[51] Likewise, and
going the other way, to limit human rights to certain human types
defined by certain ethnic, performative, racial, cultural, age or gender
conditions is, again, not a condition of misunderstanding but a meaningless employment of the concept – it carries no sense within the
language game. The criteria of use are establishing the limits of sense
here.

As having sense by virtue of its use human rights shed the universalist pretensions proffered by neo-Kantian axioms and look instead
to appropriate conditions of use. They become overtly pragmatic in
hue. The linguistic self plunges the *cogito*, the persistent subject in
its subjective world of self-consciousness, the unifying inner core of

self so vaunted by liberal human rights discourse, into the river of ordinary life. The dry banks of purity and the absolute remain for the angels alone – as humans we are consigned to go with the flow, to be buffeted by the currents of time and chance. The liberal fear is that without supposing or intuiting this non-reducible core self human identity amounts to nothing more than the random amalgam of social, historical and physical experiences to which there is little rhyme or reason. If any regularity is to be had amongst the flux, and had it must be lest we err towards the licentious and directionless world of the Karamazovs, it must come from an inner sanctum of persistent being to which rationality can tether itself, a core we ultimately accept as some perfectionist axiom.[52]

This essential spirit is an alluring figure indeed: orderly, independent, non-prejudicial, pristine, invariant and ultimately distinct from any cognitive or conative debt to 'outside' experiential forces. Nozick infers it is that aspect of us that is the object of love for, as he remarks,[53] we as people, not as an amalgam of characteristics, come to love another often despite their characteristics, 'the love is not transferable to someone else with the same characteristics. And love endures through the changes of the characteristics that give rise to it.' He then, however, goes on to ask why love is historical rather than *a priori*. This suggests an undeveloped awareness of the embedded feelings of love, feelings which whilst not collapsing into Pascal's maudlin love for borrowed qualities,[54] require a greater sensitivity to characteristics than Nozick admits. The urge to conceive of a central, unifying self in this way could as well be a symptom of vainglory and an urge for control[55] where we wish to be seen as being this or that way. There is no single justification or legitimating entity save for a skeletal chimera fit for little more than contemplation. Identity and self are aspects of the flow which we learn from, become attuned to and then move with and potentially beyond. To the extent it invokes core selves human rights discourse is bewitched by the urge to explain and know about fundamentals in terms of their being an *always* persistent thing – concluding as it does that the I is the real vessel of life. But the meaning of this statement is not the same as a non-metaphysical one; it has a different use from propositions asserting fact; it alludes to a myth which can only be shown, not explained. All we can do is show how *this* is the order of things.[56] 'My attitude towards him is an attitude towards a soul. I am not of the opinion that he has a soul.'[57] We use human rights on the grounds that this attitude is regular – it requires no explanation.

It is possible to imagine alternatives to, say, the ascription of persistent identities beyond instances of experience – for example in a world where people alternated between types; Jekyll and Hyde characters where it was the usual thing to have two names; we do not have to talk of split personality. Such a world shows how there are many uses of the word personality, none of which are philosophically privileged, 'for the ordinary use of the word "person" is what one might call a composite use suitable under the ordinary circumstances'.[58] The words self, identity, I, subject, agent do not refer to different entities as such, but are used in different ways in our language. In so imagining selves to be other than they are the naturalness of our attitude to others as though they have a soul becomes clearer. It cannot be legitimated or reasoned, nor will it always be absolute and transparent, but by envisaging the effects of things being other than they are we can confirm to ourselves things as 'they are'.

There is no absolute meaning, no legitimate heir to the concept of self save for its being something grammatically constituted in imaginative use. The link between the self, its identity, facings, practices, experiences and the like is internal – how something is being produced is inseparable from what type of thing it is. There is no meta-level operating here, hence our just having an attitude to and not an opinion (knowledge) about others. The self is not discrete but a necessary aspect of being in a world with language – it is a part of the natural and spontaneous systematic regularity that is the human form of life. It is osmotically linked to its context; but the context is likewise osmotically linked to the self – each partakes of the other in grammatical cycles of absorption and effraction. A self cannot be essentialized beyond experience, but nor can a rule or norm be essentialized beyond subjective view.

Liberal reasoning imputes a core to resist a collapse into relativism – for liberals who aspire to this throne of selfdom the idea of having to go with the flow is a crime of great enormity: the active persual of anonymity. Their supposed choice between the authority of the self or the directionless ruminations of the crowd is what is problematic here – it presupposes a private language in battle with a behaviourist spectacle; a nonsensical conflict. It is not a prior condition, nor is it an amalgam of bland Pavlovian reactions, but a grammatical prodigy set in constant relations of keeping faith with itself given existing rules, language games and forms of life. Immersed in experience, experiment and explosion – both pupil and effractor, it learns less by the repetition of assertion than a nurtured sense of appropriateness. The pupilage is very open to the influence of rhetoric and pragmatic impulse. It resists formal abstraction in favour of a focus on use, absorption and re-use.

The rules it follows under such a pupilage are enabling (the aesthetic moment where pupil takes over and becomes creator) but also encoding (the risk of nurturing paranoia, myopia or neuroses) or entropic (the inadequacy of translation in meaning from one context to another risking an ever-increasing dilution of the practice). Thus anthropological identities are at risk of collapsing into aspect blindness. To avoid this it must be clear that linguistic succour always invokes the possibility of linguistic violence – the very delineation of limits is suggestive of the question: why?

This learning procedure is political: the possibility of falling prey to rules, myth and truth that idle because of their idols, ultimate categorizations and constructions is pregnant with issues of freedom, power and rights. And so is the potential for resistance to these phantasmagorias found in *grammatical* rules, myths and truths focused on regularity and constancy in use as relational mediums which once fully absorbed spill over into individuated and thus potentially alternative grammatical rules, myths and truths. The resultant political life consists in developing an aspect awareness to acknowledge the distinction between things – in taking a second look and in re-adjusting our perspective rather than looking for nonsensical external legitimating criteria or creating hypothetical scenarios of such abstraction as alleviate us from the pain of making things fit amongst the rough ground. To be political here requires flexibility, for rather than seeking to manipulate the external in line with an internally generated blueprint of correctness, aspect seeing demands we look at things, including ourselves, from different points of view:

> If life becomes hard to bear we think of a change in our circumstances. But the most important and effective change, a change in our attitude, hardly ever occurs to us, and the resolution to take such a step is very difficult for us.[59]

It is for us to take these steps – the self, identity, facing relationship is synergistic – it involves consent, deliberative intent and commitments to such intent experienced within the forms of life which constitute not the barriers to knowledge but their conditions.[60] It is to the political resonance of these possibilities of use that human rights must focus if the onslaught upon their integrity as coherent concepts is to be shown as itself a confusion.

4 Liberal and pragmatic forms

We must make people feel obliged to us in accordance with what
they are, not we.

(Lichtenberg *Aphorisms and Letters*, Cope, 1969, p. 33)

Ethics is a condition of a changing world and not simply a comment
upon it, a world where regularity is found in resemblance rather
than essentials, where identity is a locus of absorption and effraction
rather than resistance, and where the self is less an asserted revelation
or architectural edifice than the weave of ongoing grammatical
motion. To look, then, for what is common in or about all *homo
sapiens*, a central justificatory image of a core, mental well of being
common to all human rights claimants, and to explain such entities
in terms of primitive natural laws, is to suffuse distinctions, variety
and difference in the bewitching glow of some absolute unity – a
kind of latter-day questing beast, the search for which often throws
awry the possibility of any sensitive attunement to the localized
conditions of narrative being. Rather than map foundations to our
practices, human rights, if they are to have sense, emerge as considerations to be subscribed to in such practices.[1] They can only function grammatically, and to understand their nature is to approach
them linguistically. There is no single way of insulating the concept
in some metaphysical world free from what Augustine called the sin
of time and of earthly place.

Invoking the idea of a persistent if not immutable identity is crucial
for human rights – but given the concept of linguistic self and anthropological identity the idea of this being an inner core is subsumed by
family resemblance in which the self is the centripetal force by which
the often uncertain, alluring, enigmatic and multi-faceted identities
are used with a measure of constancy. This denial of an inner subjective reality does not deny self-articulation – indeed it makes sense

of it as something which can be appreciated without any appeal to rarefied and highly abstracted planes of being. Imitation and habit are supplemented by the possibility of imagined, poetic responses which break free from a solidarity with the everyday without recourse to any external field or testimony.[2] The manoeuvre is an imaginative and gestural one in which the rules and conventions become intuitive, absorbed and reflected upon to a heightened and individuated degree.[3] This osmotic creativity of the self is not *sui generis*, but uses the exhaustion, bewilderment, attraction or subjection it experiences in one world to motivate perspectives upon others. To the extent that human rights conceive choice as constitutive of the development and *inner* commitment of some inner entity or foundational field they are incoherent. To have any substance life must have a hold of something, deep attachments to tradition coupled with equally deep revulsions. Impartiality falls foul of language games and practices. To compel life to develop an immunity from chance, luck or conflict by abstract theorizing from our ordinary selves serves only to trace an ideal reminiscent of the Papal invocations of absolute piety, humility and filial respect so reviled by Machiavelli. If human rights are to function they must meld with the multifarious practices by which many people conceive integral aspects of their character; the very real and partial reasons for their bothering to exist in the world at all.[4]

Wittgenstein likened language to a labyrinth of paths: 'You approach from *one* side and you know your way about; you approach the same place from another and you no longer know your way about.'[5] The way we explore is by cultivating the anthropological nose which lets us appreciate practices: a willingness to dispense with the reasons and even reasoning held so dear by a specific form of life in favour of making connexions and acknowledging the distinctions between them and many others. So it is in nurturing an aspectival imagination that the use of these rights seems most resonate. Whether such a role is compatible with a sustained embrace of the orthodox liberal myth from which they emerged is questionable, given their being a practice themselves.

LIBERAL MYTH

The dominant pattern to liberal theory is found in the weaving together of two central types of rights-fabric: the open and free use of critical, rational deliberation on individual interests and the good life (protected and promoted by what are misleadingly referred to as negative rights to forbearance[6]) coupled with the provision of the best possible means available to realize autonomy (ensured through the recognition of economic and social rights, those provisions emerging as necessary claims for the material well-being of peoples, and the acknowledgement of cultural or group rights which protect arenas of legitimate difference). This coupling *constitutes* practices in modern liberal democracies: individual self-understanding in a context of the mutual attribution of respect and a concern for equality[7] (a mix of Aristotle's geometric and arithmetic equality) informs the distributional and regulatory institutional structures. The hypothesis is that people have individuated rational natures, interests, desires and, due to the plurality of these interests, they must organize a system by which no one of them is unjustly prevented from articulating such interests.

The liberal idea of self is not as citizen but, foundationally, as rationally predictable self-interested chooser[8] capable of standing back and scrutinizing their context in the light of their willed integrity; without this autonomous consent practices and institutions become ethically illegitimate, imposed rather than chosen. Structural language games must be played according to rules which free and rational agents would agree to under fair and equal conditions.[9] Justice, those ethical rules most concerned with the social well-being of people, is articulated through principles which not only can be agreed to (reason) but should be agreed to (honour, good faith) on the basis of individual understanding of what constitutes their will. The institutional upshot of this is a qualitative, though often qualified, suspicion of elitist and paternalist planners in favour of the uncircumscribed and the inherently value-laden autonomous self; a focus upon impartial distributional policies which look to the conditions and not the content of expression; openness in the functioning of and access to office; and clarity, equality and consistency of law.

The myth is that of the non-reducible core to self. Stanley Benn articulates well what is a common thread: he envisages people as plan-makers in a world of plan-makers entitled first and foremost to equal respect reflected in the inevitable primacy of the negative, first-order or liberal rights to forbearance.[10] Plans are *unique* because it is through the awareness that conceptions of plans are possessed, are owned and subject to choice, amendment and criticism, that the self is able to perceive an identity over time. Projects become an accompaniment of what is innate in the self, badges of worth. What is morally important for Benn is not the content of these projects or the character of the person, but the fact that it is a project *belonging to the person.* This is the crux of modern liberal mythology: in response to the counter-intuitive conclusions reached by consequentialist utilitarian reasoning, which sees subjects solely as mediums through which values such as happiness are manifest, and so reduces issues of justice to questions of value aggregation throughout society as a whole, it postulates a dualist vision of the self – that part which chooses actions and that part which chooses what constitutes a choice of action.[11] Projects are open to change, to analysis, to revision because the subject who chooses them is capable of occupying a foundational meta-level which resounds throughout their activity. It is as a potentially separable identity that subjects come to have human rights as claims to a fundamental respect owed in the light of their being potential plan-makers. The inherent value of subjects is seen as logically distinct from the intrinsic value of their experiences: one expresses the value of worth,[12] the other that of experience, and it is only at the level of the former that value ceases to wax and wane, where all people become ethically equal in terms of autonomy and responsibility.[13] Though the content of our plans varies enormously, as do the effects of their implementation, we are all of us equal as beings who make plans for the good.

The psychological aspect of this myth stems largely from the Enlightenment's urge to invoke a growing sense of environmental control rooted in a fetishized scientistic generalization. The writings of Smith, Ricardo, Turgot and Mandeville all sought to show how habitually vicious self-concern, when institutionally acknowledged and channelled, promoted an effective and efficient public good. In conjunction with this psychological foundationalism of *libido dominandi* and the neurosis thereof appeared a forceful moral aspect informed by the Cartesian suspicion of orthodox social narratives coupled with the modernist exhortations of Kant to shed immaturity and nonage through the embrace of continual, critical self-instruction and creation, and human rights are very much creatures of this modernist taxonomy. The problem, and one Kant's third critique in contra-distinction to his advocation of noumenal being makes clear, was that such a programme of ongoing rational creativity can easily collapse into a dogmatic assertion of a universal rational standard,[14] for self-belief partakes of practice, a context.[15] It is limited in scope not by reason alone but what it makes sense to say given existing criteria of expression. To elevate self-critique into a self-legitimating, self-authenticating, self-justifying, self-validating, self-sustaining and self-legislating autonomous being is to be held in the dramatic pause of a rationalistic fiction: we are conquered by an ideal picture.[16]

This is the urge of all transcendental dogma, to persuade us of the legitimacy of a move from appearance to reality, from falsehood to truth, from evil to good, and so to ignore what Wittgenstein urged us to see – that truth is something we embody, not something outside of us which we can reach towards and only touch on occasions of brilliance, luck or divine providence. We are prone to identify auton-omy as that best representation of truth, a Being 'I' lying behind the flux of life, rather than as an expression intimately related to the immanence of creativity encountered through an immersion in gram-mar; 'I' is nothing more nor less than a grammatical convention.[17] We forget Nietzsche's insight that the means of representationalism which enabled us to escape from those very means is a masked comedy of self-interest. The self is cultivated through effective becom-ing in its cultural context, not a being isolate from it.[18] He criticized *representations* of the self not because they established identity, but because in doing so they encouraged, or bewitched, us to see such identity as truth. The liberal myth and its attendant perfectionism tends to ignore that worth resides less with divine inheritance than relations occasioned by the self in open concert with other selves;[19] and that with regard to the journey of the self through life, be it eschatological or otherwise, to travel hopefully and never arrive is itself the goal.

   The liberal mythology takes as its keystone the desire to go beyond what Castoriadis calls 'the closure of meaning'[20] created by tradi-tional forms of culture and to seek to criticize dogmatic represen-tations, yet it creates the blueprint of its own enclosure; it, as Gadamer remarks on the Enlightenment, constitutes a prejudice against prejudice. We should realize, exhorted Descartes, the Enlight-enment *Philosophes*, Kant, Mill, Green and latterly Rawls, that active citizenship can all too often be nothing more than blind adherence to dogmatic and despotic social institutions, and that to guard against this we must represent agency as self-reflective and self-referential thought[21] within social systems whose prime purpose is the provision of critical, evaluative and creative space. Society is not run along cabalistic lines where linguistic practices are soaked in runic inter-pretation and passive imitation but as an arena for the effective and efficient expression of autonomy. Yet these exhortations are as much an invocation of runes as anything else, and one of which the tradi-tional use of human rights partakes. They are the claims and duties necessary in order to ensure that all people *qua* individuals are able to attain and maintain their *own* idea of good and status in their *own* surroundings in their *own* time. Rights language does not have the purpose of establishing things as a matter of right, rather 'Rights express moral desirability *to* or *for* or *from the point of view of* some individual'.[22]

Human rights, then, are not individualistic in the sense that they perpetually fracture institutions and practices; they are a practice like any other, one which emphasizes fracture. Nor do they just require passive inaction; the duties we have to uphold rights are forceful and active. They are individualistic in the ontological sense – they take individual interests and purposes as the primary source of ethical expression, securing as they do goods for private enjoyment from public resources. They express a positive, normative commitment to what institutions ought to do, namely refrain from imposing conceptions of the good life upon others. This is a matter not of relativism or skepticism but of what it is right to resist, namely the institutional encroachment upon and unifying of language games. Liberals cannot be neutral about human rights; they see them as 'primary goods' or 'trumps' that ensure we are able to stand back from our contexts and assess how we are going, are likely to go and have gone in the light of our own standards. So whilst human rights represent no overt, comprehensive theory of a specific good (gone are the Lockean theological axioms) they do represent a very strong commitment to the idea of impartial justice. Thus, the state, as the enforcer of human rights, is urged to adopt positive stances on issues like the eradication of murder not because life is good without murder but because it infringes rights of people in possession of Kantian souls. Right has priority over good, and the rules of justice pertain to the provision, and not any recommended use, of rights.[23] In addition, then, to an explicit rejection of any apparent monolithic ethical or comprehensive ought, there is in liberalism no possible appeal to an outside referee like Rousseau's 'Supreme Legislator', able to discern the best possible course for our actions, nor is there recourse to an identified innate potential which we should be gradually unravelling through the development of 'possible intellect'. Rather, humans as rational, critically self-aware beings choose for themselves in what manner they journey through life. In so asserting liberalism focuses upon the inalienable, equal and non-derogable nature of rights, a focus which clearly favours those societies tolerant of diversity, plural in beliefs, versed in the peaceable and reasonable resolution of conflicts under the rule of law and respectful of the integrity and dignity of their autonomous members. Despite aspirations to the contrary there is an appeal to a foundational good.

This, then, is the specific deliberative heritage from which we approach human rights; one which seemingly invalidates their use as a universal system of appeal. In use they act as claims to those things it is ethically necessary to secure *to or from an individual perspective* and hence have resonance in those practices where what is of value is what is of value to individuals. Those finding this refined individualism abhorrent, or nonsensical, become strangers unable to partake of the practice and its myth. This poses something of a dilemma for the liberal impulse itself which, whilst recognizing the legitimacy of other local cultures and their peoples, is at risk in making such affirmations of rejecting its own maxims by supporting distinctly illiberal ways of life.[24] In response to this tension between toleration of what is other and the active promotion of autonomy the latter appears primary, if only because liberalism aspires to more than a *modus vivendi*. Human rights are seen to function as a way of transcending the schismatic world of insider and outsider by providing an increasingly foundational language of autonomy with a limited tolerance provided by thin or impartial theories of the good through which we cast our pleas for decency, respect and duty. It is no coincidence that the willingness with which they are being invoked by all and sundry is coupled with an expansion of liberal-democratic forms – it is less an embrace of difference than a form of life acting as a melting-pot into which alternative forms of life are thrown.

A sustained and complex version of the liberal myth is told by John Rawls and it behoves any serious attempt at showing that these theories are but tales, though tall and true, to listen in. Rawls is useful here in that through his willingness doggedly to tell, and re-tell in the light of interjections, assessments and rebuttals, there is left upon the listener a vivid impression of how things are with the liberal. In the grip of the plot the concept of the political becomes a pivotal figure – a character of decency, reasonableness and perspicuity with whom we seek dominion in well kempt bonds of constructed calm. The allure of this figure seems unproblematic for the storyteller, but on being told the story tends to an abstraction and fantasy that can be as much an exercise in escapism as it is in description.

LIBERALISM AND RAWLS

John Rawls' two principles of justice epitomize the lexical priorities of the liberal pattern.[25] As rationals with plural, civic lives we are to demand as requirements of justice a principle covering primary basic liberties, compatible with a similar scheme for all, along with a secondary principle guaranteeing equal access to institutional offices and bottom-up redistribution policies. The basic liberties, akin to emancipatory and participatory human rights when contextualized as primary goods, focus on conditions pertaining to free thought and association, the integrity of self and the liberties covered by the anonymous rule of law; conditions which Rawls sees as necessary for the two moral powers.[26] These powers are unapologetically Kantian, being 'the capacity for a sense of right and justice (the capacity to honour fair terms of co-operation and thus be reasonable), and a capacity for the conception of the good (and thus to be rational).'[27] The moral powers represent the necessary and sufficient conditions for being full and equal members of a society;[28] they ensure that people are not only moved by but act from fair and reciprocal terms and that people can form, revise and rationally pursue determinate conceptions of the good life. As such they do not define the good in any way; they are the conditions of the good, they delineate the core, irreducible self which can suffer no invasion from a *comprehensive* moral, religious or ideological notion of the good which seeks to deny all but its own existence. Rawls aches for a well-ordered society where people have different conceptions of the good and are left free to determine these conceptions for themselves; a well-ordered society being one which acknowledges and is moved by the principles of justice which set limits to the pursuit of these life plans.[29] As such the basic liberties can only be abridged by their ilk.[30] They are deontological: manifestations of the two moral powers of agents to choose (and remain distinct from) their own ends whilst recognizing a similar ability in others which evokes the duty thereby imposed on all others to recognize such powers and so restrain themselves from eroding the multiplicity which Mill likened to the free interplay of half-truths.[31]

Changing tone mid-way through his tale, with a concern and thoroughness which belies the concomitant dilution of his position, Rawls has sought to disenchant his theory; to eschew metaphysics yet still aspire to sensibly constructed political practices. This geographical shift from the realm of the intelligibly pure to that of the sensibly located has been forced upon Rawls as the implications of the initially conceived arena for the contractual generation of justice, the Original Position (OP), have seeped through into prospective use. So abstracted from the language games of political life were his hypothetical bevy of asocial, representative bargainers, being ignorant of their substantive being in all of its aspects save for the moral powers, that they resembled endlessly repeated clones capable of little more than the endless repetition of the principles of justice, like one of those dolls from which issue a stream of words when a string is pulled, Rawls crafts the OP so carefully as to yield constant, rhythmic patterns of agreement legitimated by purely rational contractors under perfect conditions of informational deprivation. The result is unsurprisingly a metaphysical creation whose purity of form is alluring but whose fragility renders it practically useless.

The new OP, developed by a number of texts,[32] is overtly a politically conceived framework; political in the sense that it turns away from the adoption of rival metaphysical positions so as to avoid any allegiances whereby a single comprehensive conception of the good (religious, philosophical or ethical) comes to dominate the social weal.[33] The new OP is a starting point for a theory which connects the political principles of justice with conceptions of citizens as free, equal, reasonable and rational beings. Rawls constructs a free-standing conception of justice where rational parties situated in and absolutely constrained by reasonable conditions (the veil of ignorance) arrive at reasonable principles of justice,[34] which are then drafted as constitutional rules, then enacted through process of legislation and finally interpreted by adjudicators.[35] This framework is informed by general information about our society and clearly involves an active appreciation of institutions (constitution, legislature, judiciary) as historical creations upon which we can reflect and act[36] and in the light of which we can assess terms of relevance and fit to the principles contractually agreed upon.[37] The resultant just constitution, then, is not a rigid creation but an ideal to be worked towards under the historical possibility of adjustment and ongoing questions of perspicuous constitutional design.[38] Rawls is appealing to a considered reflective equilibrium in judgements here, one distinct from our private judgements on our own well-being, which permits all reasonable doctrines to persist. Thus he carefully distinguishes between what Waldron calls a 'communal interest'[39] in being a member of a tolerant society, and a particular interest in being free from torture, discrimination and so on. Thus justice as fairness yields the deepest and most basic unity achievable in society, an overlapping consensus,[40] by virtue of its being exclusively focused upon those basic structures of society that all persons with command of the two moral powers would see as reasonable by virtue of publicly discussed principles.

Rawls aims, then, to create a political liberalism which, firstly, proposes fair and equal terms of social co-operation endorsed and acted upon by free and equal persons and, secondly, acknowledges the burdens (duties) of judgement and their implications for adopting comprehensive theories of the good.[41] The result is an edifice – a well-ordered society, defined as peaceful, non-expansionist institutions legitimated by the people and with a concern for basic human rights,[42] whose justification is *pro tanto*. Citizens it is hoped will always judge by their comprehensive commitments that political values normally outweigh any conflicting non-political values, it being only reasonable to endorse those constitutional procedures encountered in the tradition of common sense prevalent within well-ordered societies (fair co-operation, reasonable, rational, free and equal citizens).[43]

This narrowing of the sights of justice as fairness, Rawls suggests, is a result of a purely political conception of autonomy – something achieved by living under, acknowledging and endorsing reasonably just constitutions securing liberty and equality for all: an existential fear of the perpetual erosion of our comprehensive goods motivates a procedural inner certitude as to our duty of civility cast under the imperative of reasonableness. This purely political conception of justice, say Mulhall and Swift, reflects Rawls' belief that, assuming society is always plural and hence characterized by conflicting comprehensive doctrines partially reconcilable only through the exercise of state power, the only thing people will agree on in a minimally democratic, well-ordered and constitutional society is that institutions must coerce free and equal people in an entirely transparent manner itself controlled through the reasonable and rational mechanism of the basic liberties.[44] No longer abstract and constraining, the basic liberties do not so much control the will of the people as represent its very expression – according to the new Rawls they have no substantive status of their own, but are creations of the wide reflective equilibrium found amongst peoples. They articulate the values of emancipation (right to life, liberty and property) and participation equally. The liberties of the ancients (civic engagement) and the moderns (individualism) are lexical brothers, each is crucial in effective and efficient representation of the two moral powers. Whilst no longer universal as comprehensive goods Rawls sees their role as universalizable when constitutionalized as a law of peoples realized from a constructivist position of gradual, sequential identification with the desirability of political liberalism by rational and social agents.[45]

The OP acts heuristically to show the fundamental ideas prevalent within well-ordered societies. Rawls is not abandoning but containing his Kantian stance; he is not abandoning philosophy, but leaving it as it stands, and whilst not explicitly acknowledged by Rawls, this ensures his substantive procedural justice (favouring the liberal values of impartiality, equality, openness, lack of coercion and unanimity[46]) appeals not only on grounds of civic prudence, but the inherent value of the liberal way.[47] The principles and relations of justice are not based upon considerations of marginal utility but constituted between the wills of rational beings, albeit from historical moments, in accordance with the universal laws of freedom cast in reasonableness (morally right action being that which, if universalized, would leave intact the freedom of other rational beings). He still invokes the Kantian maxim of reflective judgement to think from the standpoint of others; this is a deep tenet of liberal being. Rawls can only acknowledge that whilst justice can no longer be premised on an order antecedent and given to us, it must relate to established public institutions, it can still be categorical from what Waldron calls the internal view,[48] from within the liberal form of life. This is experienced in his insistence that people should come to realize that although they may be committed on a private level to some fundamental background conditions of certainty whose *Weltanschauung* involves at least the partial subsuming of self to hegemonic forms, on a public level as citizens they must recognize that the political principles of justice as fairness are primary and that when in conflict such non-perfectionist goods as represented by basic democratic structures should take precedence.[49] Rather than explicitly accept the need for pragmatic principles as aspects of effective and efficient substantive narrative conditions embodied by qualitative distinctions, a kind of equality between unequals,[50] Rawls wants to confine such very real and politically relevant distinctions to what he sees as the morally irrelevant private sphere for the purposes of politics. This morally irrelevant sphere includes the social, the forming of groups for recreational or business purposes, the media and religious or ethical groupings. At the risk of sounding too astrological about this, Rawls is asking the self to act in accordance with the rising of its political aspect to the exclusion of all others. This seems akin to asking a linguistic self to focus on one aspect, to concentrate on a single path, when their identities conflate in such a myriad of ways that such self-willed myopia proves impossible to sustain given our being very much embedded in circumstance.

It is the contractual nature of the OP that remains problematic here, suffering as it does under a misconceived idea of the conditions or criteria of meaningful and regular activity. Principles of civic living do not arise as the result of contractual bargaining on universal conditions of interest reconciliation (wide reflective equilibrium) but as aspects of language games we inherit. Rawls seems uncomfortable with this anthropological 'conditioning'; the liberal paranoia of rules which mull and caul the free expressive self crafted by the two moral powers. The urge to reasonableness seems predicated on an assumption that civic rules are the necessary evil,[51] and hence must be absolutely transparent, anonymous and minimal in their exercise of power. Those principles we agree upon, then, are clear, codified and neutral – for fear of their being abused or warped we *make and ensure* them through contract, as idols of the tribe, into limiting criteria of civic being; constitutive of what it is to be a citizen; exclusionary and all-abiding conditions of acceptance to which we hope all will aspire. The rules limit us to protect us from our state of natural imperfection. Rawls' theory of political reasonableness is still caught up in the anxiety of a perceived tension between unbridled individualities in comprehensive forms and political stability, one which is calmed by the impersonal duty-bound rules of civility understood as resulting from a collective, pre-civic body of self-evident knowledge of the primacy of reasonableness. As Mulhall points out, this attenuates the self not only by restricting its civic scope to the political, but emasculating the civic world to the extent that all it can demand of the individual is compliance[52] – creativity remains an accident. But civic rules are not restrictive in this sense, nor do they somehow relieve us of the responsibility of creativity and exploration, for there is no sensible thing beyond their scope called a self or identity upon which they can potentially impose. Rules act like signposts, they are suggestive of ways of going, they provoke as much as they contain. In following rules of the language game we are taught how to grasp meaning, not how to submit to it. In learning the formulae we are able to move from the finite to the infinite, from being a pupil to being a master able to discern inventive but appropriate ways of employing rules, subject to the inevitable competing contextual considerations. This use of rules is not the result of intersubjective agreement but part of our natural history, of our being in a world with language, and so to talk of them as agreed frameworks is nonsensical and confusing – they are what enables us to go about our everyday lives, as simple as that.

But what is simple is not to be confused with what is easy. That the linguistic self uses rules to articulate the scope of its potentially dynamic identities does not mean it is continually able or even allowed (in terms of sense) to do so. We often feel so aggrieved or passionate or entrenched, especially with questions of civility, that it becomes impossible not to publicly disagree about them. Rawls' civic space wants to deny these schisms as undesirable pollutants in the alpine-fresh air of reasonable political interchange. It becomes very hard to envisage just what sort of being Rawls has in mind when he talks of people being able to at one and the same time express themselves as an integral aspect of a vibrant, dynamic and open system of linguistic rules (private or social people in command of comprehensive allegiances) *and* as citizens; as a public, civic weal, we (the Western democratic we) are all reasonable enough to agree to basic principles which, irrespective of more personal commitments, we subscribe to. As civic rule followers we often take our ethics *in toto*; people combine their ethical armoury with other forms of life and language games such that there may be family resemblances between varying conceptions of the ethical and just, but no separable, first-order conversation which somehow remains free from the trammels of narrative perspective. Antagonism and tension are necessary aspects of grammatical space within which people as language users evolve not just reasonably at a civic level but erratically, backwardly, transcendentally, imaginatively, shockingly and so on.[53] It is forms of life which render our lives coherent and consistent, which show what is to count as knowledge, as agreement, as reasonable, and these forms, which dictate the flow of action and utterance, are themselves not immutable. They do not set up an either/or framework where in failing the test of reasonableness in our discourse we fail to find a role as citizen and thence are confined to the only alternative; the perpetual silence of the non-political plains. Rawls' principles, though avowedly acknowledging historical narrative, risk imposing such a silence to the extent that they create theoretically informed, impersonal structures under the auspices of a specific substantive good – procedural liberalism, to which some aspire and others do not. Reasonableness and rationality are *moral* powers; they resonate within a specific narrative heritage of which Rawls is a pivotal element and against which we can move. Though the form of life is a point at which reasoning comes to a stop;[54] where what is embodied is commitment to constituted forms of rationality, they themselves can be the subject of change – we can *imagine* what it is like to play a different language game or for the facts to buck and a form of life be otherwise.

Rawls, as with everybody, makes judgements from within and through existing institutions, language games without which the idea of judgement would itself be meaningless.[55] We can only ever refer our actions back to the historical specificity of other actions which themselves are only recognized to the extent that other people express them through their engagement with the regularities of other forms of life. Reasonableness itself is part of what the agent is committed to. As citizens people are not private individuals able to desist from expressing themselves through certain comprehensive moral forms of life because on occasion they must act publicly, but individuals *because* they engage in forms of life using the conceptual apparatus of language users. There is in emphasizing the linguistic a move away from the substance of procedure and towards what Castoriadis sees as a more 'substantive democracy', a substance of human type, which recognizes that rather than having highest-order interests which are primarily personal people not only formulate their interests through public action (reasonableness), they live through the creative fields afforded them by forms of life woven and re-woven as aspects of their being for which they are continually responsible. By theorizing the role of citizen into a spartan conception of the political in order to maintain the appearance at least of the universalist appeal of basic liberties Rawls is invoking a stunted view of self immune from, because not engaged with, the very real ethical and religious fractures of ordinary political life. Without feelings of 'courage, responsibility and shame' consequent upon the ebb and flow of grammatical being the citizen is less a life force than a forced life unable to prevent 'the "public space" becom[ing] an open space for advertising, mystification and pornography'.[56]

Rawls is not wrong in his invocation of the two moral powers but confusing in his limiting of the idea that language is both constitutive of, and constituted to, the private sphere, preferring to impose the idea of reasonableness as necessary in the public one, when such a division, even on his own terms, conflates the idea of how we are to go about living together as inheritors and creators of differing language games and forms of life, with the idea of necessary principles of action applicable to all language users sought outside of the expression of any one form of life. The latter can, and has, led to uniformity and claims of ideological supremacy because it claims an anthropological advantage which seeks to pass judgement upon the practices in which we engage, when really such principles are grammatical expressions, internal to how we are. Rawls' idea of reasonableness acts as a constraint in the OP, the implication being that such a language game is played and ended at will,[57] whereas it can just as well be an enabling good which partially constitutes that will. Rawls' liberalism has shifted foundational authority, it has not challenged it; and its invocation of reasonableness is as much an aspect of what Castoriadis calls the instituting of socially imaginary significations[58] wrought in the already socially instituted as any other form of principled justification. Therefore 'what we have to do is analyse specific rationalities rather than always invoke the progress of rationalization in general'.[59] Knowledge, power and the like circulate in institutions which are themselves expressions of individual and collective commitments.

PRAGMATIC LIBERALS

Basic liberties operate as ideal constraints on exploration, not enablers – they are constructions of control, warnings that meditations upon the high command of procedure must always run between the established banks of such a procedure, a framework, lest they overflow, lose definition and dry up. The result is less governance in use than government in blueprint sustained by a collective, impersonal devotion to procedure[60] mustered by the folk on the theoretical hill.

If not theoretically, then grammatically. Shifting from the construction of frameworks designed to contain and emphasize specific elements of human action in biographical ideals, to a description of how it is we go about our ordinary activity as autobiographical subjects capable of rendering to ourselves and others contextually sensitive and appropriate descriptions of how we are with the world, requires of political concepts like human rights an attunement to inherent differences in airs and substantive values. Less symbols of the immutable, ideal or preferable, they become tools with a myriad of uses, some of which are more appropriate than others, used in moments of threat, courage and effort felt in the continual development of experience and imagination.

The qualms thereby articulated are well expressed by Elizabeth Wolgast in her discussion on the position of women in the workplace where equal rights legislation, which supposedly ensures that no one is discriminated against because of their sex, conceives conception, birth and rearing of children as a burden to be overcome rather than a strenuously productive period of revelatory value reorientation.[61] The entire emotional gamut of the maternal experience is equated with a service rendered, compensated for and alleviated in order not to hamper long-term competitiveness in the fight for office. Difference is eradicated by postulating some form of veil of ignorance behind which more and more of us are to sit, when this difference is the very condition rights seek to emphasize. Invoking Wittgenstein's description of grammatical truth conditionals has far-reaching implications for politics, requiring of it a relinquishing of obscurantist generalizations and idealizations which we either conquer or to which we succumb, in favour of seeking knowledge and judgement from within existing criteria. Creating artificial, abstract states of innocence and perfection is tantamount to wickedness for it absolves us from the tragedy of our partiality, our becoming, our being creatures in possession of a language through which we are able, in coming face to face with others who act in ways that we do, to witness an understanding of who we are in which we can take delight, be indifferent or even shudder with disgust.[62]

The risk encountered by this annihilation of a potential arena of homogeneity and equality in which repose can be found is the despair so trenchantly felt by the Elder Zossima in the *Brothers Karamazov*. The absence of foundations consequent upon a language capable only of a self-referential assertiveness, is that duty, principle and right become matters of habit to be bandied about at one's convenience and ignored in the depths of one's despair. It is exactly this kind of sceptical *reductio* that Rawls is attempting to avoid in his separation of the political from the private; but one which serves only to restate foundationalism in a round-about manner with a weak sense of duty-bound integrity manifest in reasonableness. In leaving philosophy as it is Rawls is ignoring, but not dispensing with, the revelatory aspect of metaphysics – the world can still be split between diversionary, fluffy aesthetics and fundamental, undistorted political morality. The basic liberties inhabit the realm of what is revealed right as distinct from the dissolution of ordinary life.

PRAGMATIC PERSPECTIVES

Richard Rorty looks to the Damocles effect of this rift in being with an iconoclastic disdain. Rawls is forgetting that liberalism is not a doctrine of clarity at all, it is a pragmatic praxis which need not embroil itself in scholastic meanderings; leave that for the irrelevants. Embracing the intra-linguistic nature of truth as investigated by the likes of Wittgenstein, James and Dewey, the ethnocentricity of human perspectives, and the bundle of sentential attitudes cemented by contingent beliefs and rules of practice that is the human self, we are to revel in the casting off of universalist, abstract shrouds and stand proud in our 'fuzzy' de-philosophized nakedness. The search for theoretical purity is meaningless: 'there is no natural order of justification and beliefs, no predestined argument to trace.'[63] The way out from the fly bottle, how we go about solving problems and making nonsense apparent rather than the search for what we should be, is secured by coherent adaptations to specific environments manifest in regular and successful interactions.[64] Politics is not an arranging, ordering, structuring science disclosed by philosophical reflection but the practice of political problem-solving whose principles are reminders of such efforts, *and not abstracted supports for them.* Foundationalist vocabularies such as human rights discourse are in fact 'just another set of little human things'[65] which we use as part of a contingent language. Pragmatists like Rorty are aspiring to be honest here: they justify values such as toleration, autonomy and openness not on the basis of a blueprint, but as practices which work well in their established modes of expression. We justify all aspects of our living on the basis of how they help us organize our activity and anticipate our experiences.

> We should restrict ourselves to questions like 'Does our use of these words get in the way of our use of those other words?' This is a question about whether our use of tools is inefficient, not a question about whether our beliefs are contradictory.[66]

How we are to proceed politically, then, is governed by the rational and epistemic authority encountered in the regular activity of conditioned agents infused with established modes of common sense. Rorty is concerned with surfaces – the melding and welding of arenas of action for which there are no foundations save for the solidarity of contentment and acceptance.

The human self shares such planar characteristics. Pragmatism is not a theory on human nature, but an articulation of how we constitute and become constituted as constellations of convictions encountered under grammatical description. There is no essence, the self

> is a network that is constantly re-weaving itself in the usual Quinean manner – that is to say not by reference to general criteria (for example rules of meaning or moral principles) but in a hit-or-miss way in which cells re-adjust themselves to meet the pressures of the environment.[67]

The weaving and adjustment are suggestive of a vagueness and reflectiveness which permeates Rorty's view of the self, a condition exploited by creative re-description allowing new, alluring, repulsive, strange and tangential workings of the rules we inherit as language users. The use of rules is as much about the exploration of alternatives as it is further initiation in the orthodox. Hence the importance of discursive[68] links and narrative for Rorty – rather than philosophize we are to use metaphor to explore the space for re-definition left by the inevitability of possible further interpretation.[69] Autonomy is characterized not by the absence of cultural influence but in how we use our cultural background in creative self-expression. It is not a question of going beyond grammar but exploring its limits; this is how we seek to define our selves.[70]

Such radical redescription is not open to us all – indeed the abrasive force of a continual awareness of and challenge to the contingency of our position is a force few can bear. Those whose identity resides in a struggle with and recoiling from final solutions Rorty calls ironic poets;[71] an iconoclastic self 'trying to get out from under inherited contingencies and make his own contingencies'.[72] They are ironic about specifics; dispensing with metaphysical purity they wrestle with *Fortuna* and *necessita*, what Rorty calls 'time and chance', rather than trying to avoid or ignore them.[73] It seems that through this ironic progress ironists embrace the potential for betterment without becoming too certain and static.[74] Such imaginative manipulation of the historically contingent brings with it the possibility of new conceptual novelties to shift the focus of language games. The created aesthetic values are neither transcendent nor rigorously logical but sporadic and fused through family resemblances which are subsequently unravelled by the grammatical redescriptions of yet other aesthetic heroes.

Irony is something Rorty identifies as inwardly creative and socially forceful; reversing the liberal public/private distinction he argues that autonomy is not the sort of thing that can be embodied in social institutions as indicative of freedom;[75] liberty is present in the recognition of one's contingent position, it is a felt experience expressed allegorically and metaphorically in an urge to overcome, a continual revelling in the will to struggle (which is at constant risk of forgetting the will to live);[76] a glorification of the perpetual challenge which pragmatism, a consciously practical doctrine, would eschew. Strong poets mobilize grammatical resources for an ironic destiny conceived privately; at the public level of the *conscience collective* they remain infused with a sense of decency, responsibility and a practical urge to harmonize inevitably conflicting interests. Rorty invokes a divided self, but one which is a consciously pragmatic acknowledgement and not a foundationalist essence of core integrity, worth or dignity. Aesthetics is for the delectation of the

private; politics is about the effective and efficient institutional ordering of public relations in line with established narrative, common
sense and felt pragmatic intuitions and experiences. Rather than
waste time seeking justifications the resultant machinery concentrates
exclusively upon the alleviation of the cruelty consequent upon being
forced to accept descriptions from another; a linguistic tyranny which
leads to the pain of humiliation.[77] As public selves we are able to
appreciate, by virtue of our developing a sentimental education, how
the other is a continuing aspect of ourselves, how others though different are not non-human but beings with friends, mothers, homes
and the like, who feel pain like ourselves. The political problem is
not one of humans maltreating humans but of some humans failing
to recognize the humanity in others.[78] Should this socialization stray
into the private realm it should be resisted at all costs lest it stifle
the possibility of poetic self-assertion and encourage the humiliation
of being defined by others. As linguistic creatures we define our individuality through commitment to language games, none of which
should be seen as privileged. Language games vary in terms of perspicuity, efficiency, vision but not in terms of their being able to
access 'outside' reality.

The ideal citizen is a liberal ironist. Ironic because, according to
Rorty, continual imaginative encounters of identity with a myriad of
possible futures promotes the dialectic of vocabulary above propositions of logic and metaphysics, re-description above inference and
hope above assertion in order 'to make the best selves for ourselves
we possibly can'.[79] Liberal because publicly it evokes a certain kind
of knowhow, an 'ability to grasp the function of many different sets
of words'.[80] It is from these little human things, these pieces of text
that solidarity is constructed and re-constructed; solidarity is not
found, or revealed or discovered, but worked at continually. Solidarity has little to do with the two moral powers, with laws of the
universe or with a supreme moral good; it is an accumulated achievement of a people *in situ*, a Burkean prejudice. We decide to stay
liberals not because we are committed to an abstract metaphysics of
rights but because it promotes a tolerance amongst pluralities,
diminishes cruelty, promotes government by consent, is materially
very successful at problem-solving and, above all, sees truth as the
outcome of free and open discussion over time – a process rather
than a state.[81] Moving from the priority of truth to that of freedom,
liberalism allows individuals to use narrative to attempt to persuade
grammatical rivals[82] without risking any concomitant forced narrative imprisonment. Articulating established shared feelings, a

Rawlsian reflective equilibrium set without the theoretical relief, Rorty's pragmatic liberalism seeks a balance between the private articulation of autonomy manifest in irony with a public need for stability and the avoidance of pain. Indeed Rorty claims that this is exactly what Rawls is doing, generalizing from established ways of being to better show how things are with the liberals. Justice becomes a first principle because we have grown used to having a society which sees its main motivation as the reconciliation of individual, autonomous actions through various values such as toleration and social institutions such as the market mechanism and constitutional government.[83]

Rorty is not, then, pessimistic about our condition. He infuses his work with an Enlightenment bravado without invoking the foundational mush, challenging as he does not only those who attempt to seek a consensus upon rational, logical and ethical lines by theorizing either on the innate or the sublime, but also those wilting with postmodern resignation in the heat of performative contradiction and relativism. Rorty's liberalism is challenging. Limits are established by a refusal to countenance the utterances of tyrants, of the mad and of bigots as arguments which require negotiation – for them there is no refuge to be had in the dialectics and pragmatism of ironic liberal space. Rorty accepts this perfectionism as necessary, despite his belief that it may lead to irreparable schisms in outlook: the self as historically contingent will encounter others so alien as to make universal agreement impossible and undesirable.[84] As a good liberal Rorty will come across those perpetually in the shadows of their monolithic theories and strenuously deny the relevance of their kingdoms of darkness to his own narrative; they do not belong in the pragmatic liberal reflective equilibrium, whereas we adherents of limited tolerance and pragmatic problem-solving, it seems, do, in so far as we temper our aspirations in the opacity of hope.

5 Irony and the art of living

> In love, in art, in avarice, in politics, in labour, in games, we study to utter our painful secret. The man is only half himself, the other half is his expression.
>
> (Ralph Waldo Emerson 'The Poet' in Carl Bode (ed.) *The Portable Emerson*, Penguin, 1981, p. 243)

PRAGMATIC TRUTH

For now, to entertain the comforts of liberal living free from guilt is to be a pragmatic liberal.[1] As siblings to their parental, constitutional narratives liberal selves, fortuitously born amongst those narratives whose capacity for efficient and effective material control has placed them at the top of the Social Darwinian league, are versed in a Vulgate justice. The rules that guide and the ties that bind have as their motive aspect neither universal reason nor Cartesian scepticism but a volitional-will-in-grammatical-context. Language lives like a coral reef, a life which takes shape as the result of a vast and shifting number of contingencies, where new metaphors feed off and replace old ones through occupation of available or created niches.[2] Being Darwinian the pragmatic liberal looks to the interactions of a language using organism, to see 'beliefs as adaptions' rather than the Cartesian's perspective on beliefs as 'quasi pictures'.[3] The search for a universal language of representation, for an essentialist, knowing, core self and for foundational principles of justice is the stuff of fantasy. The pragmatic liberal dissolves 'objects into functions, essences into momentary foci of attention, and knowing into success at reweaving a web of beliefs and desires into more supple and elegant folds'.[4] Their will-in-context shifts with the ebb and flow of habitual, uncontroversial and familiar rule following, occasionally losing sight of the criterial limits in moments of novel metaphorical insight brought on by encounters with the unfamiliar or with the familiar from novel perspectives. But this radical re-description is the province of the ironic; for the most part we are unaware of limits as limits and are happy to play established language games. If this results in a society which MacIntyre has criticized as being the province of the manager, the aesthete and the analyst, types almost sinister in their philosophical lightmindedness, superficiality, programmed uninterestingness, and their depressingly spineless willingness to grant the presence of 'despicable types' for the sake of political freedom,[5] then so be it. 'For Dewey', Rorty approvingly cites, 'communal and public disenchantment is the price we pay for individual and private spiritual liberation'[6] and 'even if the typical character types of liberal democracies *are* bland, calculating, petty and unheroic the prevalence of such people may be a reasonable price to pay for political freedom'.[7] Embracing 'banalization' is far less risky than occasioning metaphysical darkness; besides there is always the possibility of the imaginative grammatical heroics of the poet whose novel attempts at sensitizing us to pain and humiliation, at self-creation, at re-definition, can eventually be held fast in the slowly calcified growth of criterial being, thereby benefiting us all.

Rorty has a kind of metaphorical replacement operating here. Unable to step outside of a language (Davidson) which is inherently historicized and contingent (Heidegger),[8] an ironist exists in a perpetual state of ambiguity as regards their relation to their final vocabulary, the points at which justifications and reasons for identities just come to an end in a localized common sense. Whilst convergence between theories is an impossibility, there being no absolute rational paradigm, ironists re-describe in the hope of initiating changes to the Vulgate that will bring about a world more at ease with itself; a less painful world. It is a metaphysics of rhetoric and dialectic manifest in the re-creation, revision, re-contextualization and re-description of clashing vocabularies. There is nothing beyond these vocabularies, echoing Wittgenstein's comment: 'My *life* consists in being content to accept many things.'[9] Rorty sees pragmatism as being in the business of acknowledging the points at which our spades turn. Ambiguities and angst can only be assuaged by encounters with other vocabularies, by 'enlarging our acquaintance'[10] – an inter-subjective communication between beliefs – any search for a beyond being fallacious. Hence the importance of literature and literary criticism for Rorty, engaging as they do in all manner of perspectives on possible worlds the literary enables us to conceive of the strange, the different and unfamiliar. This is a central insight on

Wittgenstein's part. Constraints are imposed by expressions of the speaker and are not determinable outside of those expressions; they embody identity. We can imagine realms where people have developed completely different ways of looking at the world but in doing so we must understand that it is not the same world at which they are looking. In so envisaging these radically different realms the naturalness of our own world and concepts is brought home to us – we come to realize just how inseparable are our concepts and our world.

Focusing upon irony, as opposed to transcendent and transcendental metaphysics, requires from us nothing more than the hope for a cruelty-free, leisured life and an acknowledgement that goodness or truth are whatever is the historically contingent consensus. There is no distinction between justification and truth here, no way of distinguishing between the way the world is from thinking this is the way the world is,[11] no one thing which makes an action or position right, for given enough stage setting anything can be made to accord with anything else. To have a point a concept must have a use, a non-metaphysical goal, of which there can be many. All representations have evaluative aspects, all actions have contextual leanings, all truths are expediencies, all objects have fictional lives[12] and all knowledge is the acquisition of perspicuous habit.[13] The pragmatist focuses on forms of justified beliefs, prejudices and traditions. The human self is an entity which adjusts in accordance with context using words not as representations of reality but as tools which once mastered are to be employed. Providing at the level of the political we ensure liberty is paramount, ethics takes care of itself.[14] Beyond this hope lies only speculative indulgence in supposed absolutes. Rorty seems to recognize that through persistence, luck, errors and repeated attempts,[15] we can come to understand the actions of others, that there are common actions, for example wanting to achieve a basic subsistence,[16] but says such common practices are not in themselves enough to create a commonality between people. That this understanding actually occurs, and thence leads to mutual respect, remains but a hope, which is all people use to bind their relations and give force to their actions.

The institutional strength emerging from this resides in slipperiness. Ideology is not met with its ilk, but with a refusal to engage; a weak attack whose lack of interest is irresponsible only to those metaphysicians who fake knowledge of there being a universal, rational 'theoretical glue'. Pragmatists refuse to get flustered by what is irrelevant. Rorty is following Rawls' emphasis on 'reasonably concrete, optimistic, plausible *political* scenarios, as opposed to scenarios about redemption beyond the grave'.[17] The ideal liberal society would be one where though distinct in degree the ironists and the masses would share narrative commitments to nominalism and historicism – if sliced up the self would be contingent right the way through. Any doubts to their being would involve the exploration of alternatives, not the assertion of justifications, and liberalism is the best kind of social life-boat[18] because as a system it best allows such an exploration. Irony is confined by liberalism; politics as solidarity cannot co-exist with the continual barrage of doubt fuelled by irony. If we were merely amalgams of linguistic flow awaiting constant re-description the concept of collectivity and identity would become nonsensical, and for this reason Rorty invokes the non-linguistic capacity to feel pain as that which gives us a grip on the idea of an embedded self with social responsibilities. Pure ironists are too narcissistic to give credence to this, but many writers and philosophers do explore the very public ambience of the cruelty and humiliation felt in the face of compulsory re-description. Picking up on the potency of the victims' anguish, fear and humiliation consequent upon hypocrisy, self-deception, greed, sadism[19] and slaughter identified by Judith Shklar as the *summum malum*,[20] Rorty thinks it indispensable to the liberal ironist to avail themselves of as many alternative final vocabularies as is possible, for only then is an understanding of the many possibilities of humiliation experienced. What unites is not a common denominator but a susceptibility to pain and a sharing of a hope for its future alleviation. We have no essential *reason* for this to be theorized over; reason is nothing more than making sense of oneself. We need only the imagination to conceive of another's pain and humiliation in being made to recognize themselves as grammatically incoherent, as being broken into mental shards, to appreciate the desirability of what Rorty terms an expanded we-consciousness, a mutual sensitivity to cruelty.

So receiving an invitation to attend the Rortyan 'at home' liberal gathering is one made attractive not merely because of its Social Darwinian credentials, nor just because it accepts conflicting aesthetic projects and so accommodates rather than quashes self-description, but because its stable direction is brought on by the successive avoidance of cruelty through the promotion of freedom above truth in an expanding we-consciousness. Though on the private level liberal pragmatists may wish for an open, tolerant society, on a public level they inhabit a moral cul-de-sac of the regular recognition of and collective challenge to instances of cruelty. Orthodoxies from other cul-de-sacs which seek to place claims of knowledge above facts of power, to put meta-ethics before sentimentality, to put truth before hope, and to put essences before cultures are outmoded, empty husks that have had their day and wait only to wither in the heat generated by the efficacious production of wealth and forged tolerance from the liberal furnace. Ironists must at least publicly remain hopeful as to an eventual abandonment of cruelty; irony must be delineated by this expanding we-consciousness; difference is thereby contained by a concern for the humiliation and pain of enforced metaphor. The public–private distinction is made sense of by a move from the question of whether we share the same final vocabulary to the question of whether we can feel pain;[21] politics should be entirely disposed to ask the latter, and ironic re-description confined to the former.

Less buffeted than annihilated by this pragmatic attack human rights as universal, foundational principles are nothing more than the outmoded whimperings of defeated, feeble metaphysicians. Worthy only of a world besotted with now irrelevant questions of an ontological nature, their ilk no longer fits in the Protean world of self-shaping, twenty-first century, aestheticized selves[22] where the focus is very much on making ourselves stronger in ourselves, more self-conscious and less concerned with affecting an attitude of superiority to others. Rawls' basic liberties are not foundational. They are aspects of a reflective equilibrium and overlapping consensus which well describe what we Western liberals are getting up to – developing a growing sense of feeling for each other as humans, rather than geeks, dikes, untouchables, wops, loonies and other pseudo-human 'types', using a Humean sentimental education. Those refusing, ignoring or failing to comprehend this political sensitivity versed not in depth but the surface similarities of the everyday (playing ball, weeping, having mothers, working, friendship) are not to be treated as irrational, as requiring just a little more instruction in the one way, but as in possession of a deprived narrative heritage of security and sympathy.[23]

Rorty is under no illusion as to the manifest difficulty of establishing the trust necessary for such sensitivity to persist – indeed he believes it is beholden on humanity to wait for a gradual cessation of humiliation from the powerful. There are no unconditionals, no arrows of absolute knowledge flying fully formed from some Goddess's bow with which to pop the megalomaniacal; to suppose there are is to suffer from resentment at being reliant on the contingent, the accidental and the genealogical. All we can do is to 'imagine that'; to invoke a fiction of involvement and not a fantasy of the pure, and leave it at that.

PRAGMATIC ELITISM

With the public–private split Rorty conjures up a restrained hero who works away at the interface of common sense and rhetorical enquiry; a sort of *Übermensch* who does the washing up. Despite contingency being so apparent, and despite their being very refined creatures whose residual interest in the humdrum lives of ordinary people must be of a suspiciously low intensity,[24] they are still, says Rorty, to be committed to the liberal system out of an acknowledgement of pain and the urge to widen further their own vocabularies best sated in a system materially efficient and effective. Rorty says at the public level the poetic champions will not only compose but be actively moved by a feeling of solidarity in the drive to avoid the pain of humiliation. But this movement is made by these connoisseurs of narrative diversity alone, whilst the rest of us linguistic epsilons, those content to wallow in their final vocabularies, merely follow, eventually arriving at a narratively accommodated version of a specific strong poet's version of self-assertion.

The struggling and prevailing grammatical hero is central for Rorty; Wittgenstein, on the other hand, placed no such faith in the manoeuvrings of poetic 'genius', preferring to be suspicious of all who would evoke the loyalty of others or wish for the lead of the great. Re-description does not require genius; all language users can do it by following and hence embodying different rules, rules which they find forced upon them. Becoming unemployed, undergoing bereavement, learning you have cancer, childbirth, suffering from stress, fleeing in the face of fear are all possible arenas of re-description which rely less on the suave, consummate and idiosyncratic use of a dictionary than the basest of survival skills. Rorty's re-descriptive poet is surely one way of changing established myths, but rhetoric is not alone; structural forces as lines of power and accidental and chaotic shifts in environmental, physical and psychological context also constitute a bucking of the facts. Take the new nomads of the tarmac as an instance. During the 1980s, in response to urban decay, family schism, personal loss, health 'problems', or even vague philosophical musings on new Aquarian dawns and the frankly unlikely re-emergence of the Isle of Avalon somewhere in the vicinity of Bognor Regis, swelling groups of travellers began to roam Britain and Ireland, living in all manner of benders and vehicles (ironically a lot of them *ex officio,* ambulances, post office vans, army trucks and the like). They constituted amongst themselves and their dogs, with hardly a strong poet in view, a fundamental narrative re-description, given testament by the almost rabid response with which their presence was met by the decent and orthodox sedentary populace. Despite the hostility and the very active efforts of a government who likened them to the bands of mediæval brigands and de-frocked clergy celebrated in the *Carmina Burana* they have managed to sustain and continually redefine themselves. But this new form of life was less the result of a continual narcissistic union with self-doubt than a necessary reaction to a very real problem, and though peppered with poetry is more substantially a movement grounded in the need for material alternatives. Though sympathetic to life as problem-solving Rorty seems confused as to who actually gets it done; seemingly limiting it to the few when it can be done by all language users.[25]

Although there is no project, conception of the good or life plan without a language in which to express them, and languages are undoubtedly influenced by the radically re-described experiences of its most gifted exponents, there is likewise no such interchange without the active participation of others in the language games. Forced re-description of the self is a source of humiliation and oppression; it involves the binding of personalities and of groups, one which it is possible to undo through active re-description using language games. But why do we have to wait for a strong poet to turn up before we make the attempt at novel, emotional, ethical and even common-sense responses? There seems to be a confusion about how the poet is to influence the grammatical form here. Reflection on forms is artistic in that it points not to a defined but an imagined use of rules.

> For instance, at my level the Pauline doctrine of predestination is ugly, nonsense, and irreligious. Hence it is not suitable for me, since the only use I could make of the picture I am offered would be a wrong one. If it is a good and godly picture, then it is so for someone at quite a different level, who must use it in his life in a way completely different from anything that would be possible for me.[26]

Thus we stand in relation to the gospels not as historical revelations nor rational truths but as myth. This contingency, however, is not a question of following where others lead. In no way did Wittgenstein see rule following as a passive activity where we just sit back and let the tide of cultural practice wash over us, following without thinking. We follow a rule blindly, but out of habit, tradition, feeling and education, not necessity. Wittgenstein wanted to show us that the differences, the manner in which we could generate infinite sentences from finite grammatical rules is something based on the ever-present possibility of re-description, the seeing of new aspects, whilst never attempting to sow the seed of a totalizing autonomy.

Surely any language user has the potential to become acutely sensitive to their narrative condition by continually questioning the legitimacy of moves in language games whilst retaining a sense of responsibility for any moves that they may wish to make of their own accord. Active self-assertion involves a constant re-evaluation of identity from positions of critical distance: we are not just to wallow in the passive remembrance of things past[27] but be alive to the possibility of defining and re-defining grammatical positions. Historical narrative and the fictional have a tendency to encapsulate the attempts of people to throw off the grammatical yoke in the exploits of a hero. Just as metaphysics essentializes, so fiction can heroicize, and that is its risk, not a reality. Allured by the splendour, eccentricity and brilliance of the aesthetic master we are prone to forget that what sustains this display is the community of ordinary language users at large, who themselves are capable of radical shifts, though in often prosaic, almost dun shades, and upon whose capacity for absorption and responsiveness the hero relies.[28] To appropriate and warp orthodox meanings requires a sense of appropriateness, a responsiveness to ordinary language and its rules.

PRAGMATISM AND SCHISM

Though linguistic selves cannot be said necessarily to meld with patterns of social action made dominant purely by the efforts of ironic poets, it may still be observed that, this being the case in many instances of playing language games, the majority are content to ape the world rather than create it. Given an awareness of the oft-found heroic element, Rorty may defend pragmatic liberalism through its containment and effective use of the heroic; the hero is not something to be effaced, resisted, thwarted, but used. Once ensconced in the guise of grammatical reputation the general hero becomes overtly self-conscious and manipulative, attempting to re-enchant the world with their own vision. Rorty chooses *poetic* heroes precisely because of this worry; being poetic the hero contains and projects their irony onto their private selves. But there is only a weak recognition here of the dangers inherent in *any* appeal to the heroic. Nurturing irony and sentimentality is itself a project at risk of becoming a projectile to be aimed at the idea of the other. Thus the liberal form of life can itself become unsentimental, its adherents thinking themselves possessed of a coherent, single outlook, free from contradiction. This absolute commitment to the we-consciousness of liberal values brought on by heroic mystification displays a singular lack of schismatic and structural acknowledgement, provoking an almost surreal idea of what it is to be a political being; one for whom one's most passionate and burning ironic explorations fold and melt over the branches of the arboreal[29] liberal structure, pliant appendages to a stratified process beyond which lies nothing but humiliation. The political is at risk of becoming little more than a filial adherence to abstracted procedure, empty of purpose.

Rorty sees the invocation of terms like inherent dignity or universal worth used in support of the existence of species-wide *ethical* constraints such as innate rights as at best mystical abstractions and at worst mawkish gush, yet his own defence of liberalism as that most efficacious of institutional systems, the product of a proud and upstanding narrative tradition seems no less romanticized; relying as it does for the sustenance of a social glue on nothing more than a solidarity built around a hope for the steady prevention of cruelty brought about by the missionary spread of an education in the surface similarities of our 'sentimental' attachments.[30] This education seems not only a rather resigned way of treating social problems but one potentially insidious in its myopia, for it amounts to advocating that we should almost forget that it is we as *individuals*, consciously committed to social institutions, who ensure the stability of any sentimentality. It tends to weaken liberalism by seeing it as something better than but irrelevant for 'outsiders'. Rorty invokes monolithic narrative, painting a scenario of conflicting 'concrete' forms of life based upon *intra*-cultural public consensus. Each culture is dominated by a type of discourse which governs the ascription of rational and ethical behaviour, and as soon as a dissenter arises, then after the requisite attempt at accommodation they are either expunged from the group as someone lacking the essential characteristics of a social being, or they sew the seeds of a new paradigm. This ethical narcissism sees modern, Western, liberal democrats as wanting to create a tolerant society of mankind, who, through persuasion rather than force, will realize an ever more inclusive society which 'constantly changes to accommodate the lessons learnt from new experiences'.[31] Such an organic unity is not recognizing plurality between cultures, it is asserting itself against those who seek to deny the orthodoxy of a moral and political system based on tolerance. It is the kingdom of Nietzsche's Last Man who eschews the hard for the warm, the enemy for the neighbour, the foolish for the wary, the worker for the entertainer, the quarrelsome for the healthy.[32] Suffering is to be annulled and happiness anointed; the human condition aspires to a tepid amniosis of complacency, a duvet world. This may well be a perspicuous viewpoint for those so insulated and hence free from the often stunting conditions of Western democratic living experienced variously in conditions of perpetual debt and the risk of material collapse, of the increasingly hazy distinctions between real and unreal in Western myth, of exposure to neurosis and hatred, of an increasingly fragile environmental homeostasis, and of persistent conditions of exploitation. But for the runts of the liberal litter, for the dispossessed and the never-connected, an apparently happy state of tolerant, free and materially comfortable living is a general aspiration whose myopia is to be resented and whose effects are to be regarded with unbridled horror.

Rorty's eulogy of sentimentality seems to be undermining his own precepts. Every evaluative judgement upon the attitudes of another form of life has to be taken using an historically embedded language which is itself part of specific forms of life, there being no meta-narrative with which we can evaluate others' practices. The drawing upon one's own *Weltanschauung*, the use of a background against which we distinguish between truth and falsity, the self as grammatical creation, is not, as Rorty seems to think it is, merely a question of plausible social construction. The self is an aspect of living in a world with language which evokes a continual process of effraction and absorption with narratives, one in which the re-figuration and consolidation of identities takes place in conditioned and conditioning relations to phenomenal conditions. Developing an anthropological sensibility is not about a subject embodying a private vocabulary – the whole project of private language is in double jeopardy. Firstly, isolate arenas of grammatical self-creation, even those of ironic doubt, are never *sui generis* and, secondly, the background conditions of certainty by which the capacity for doubt becomes sensible are not always so clear as to provide an absolute court of public appeal as to where we should go; indeed the more apparent are standards of certainty the more abstract and hence less relevant they are.

When we talk of language as a symbolism used in an exact calculus that which is in our mind can be found in the sciences and in mathematics. Our ordinary use of language conforms to this standard of exactness only in rare cases.[33]

Language is characterized as inherently open given its being unrepresentable and so linguistic selves are never subject to a complete and coherent system of rules which can be theorized about, be they steeped in private irony or public sentimentality.[34] Wittgenstein's scenario is of people playing the game according to the rules, technique and purpose, or, alternatively, of opting not to play; because of a feeling of discomfort they fail to grasp or assimilate the rules and try to resist and invent new ones. In this flux of active being and becoming, where signs and signification are in imaginative relations with pupils and masters as signified and signifiers the poetic is never confined to the private; it can always be seen as having an active, public presence. Certainty is found in a trust, in an absence of doubt, which is not based upon agreement in opinion or values but in action:

> We should sometimes like to call certainty and belief tones, colourings of thought, and it is true that they receive expression in the *tone* of voice. But do not think of them as feelings which we have in speaking or thinking.
> Ask not: 'What goes on in us when we are certain that . . . ?' but: How is 'the certainty that this is the case' manifested in human action?[35]

Selves issue the despotic demand that their thoughts and intentions must follow from their state of intending, people know that they are following a rule and are certain as to the contents of that rule, not because they are able to look inside themselves and check but because they *naturally* express themselves in a way that others understand, in a manner where there is a regular connection of the type: 'p'–p–p, which is open to interpretation from others. We are already agents with a propensity to act in a logical manner. Castoriadis explains this point in terms of creative roots, the creation always being in a relation with that which always already is, a relation which depends upon *what* is created in terms of historical practice/institution/object.[36] The ironic poet, as much as anyone else, has a vocabulary which is part of an established narrative; to criticize the old ways we use language which is built upon them.[37] To overcome problems and confusion we do not construct totally new languages, new theories, but adapt language so as to view the problem from a different aspect, which manifests itself in further narrative – there is no confining it to an entirely private mode of contemplation.

Schisms feature in this creative flow because grammatical practices lack an over-riding, single, intellectual authority able to bestow definite, coherent and single purposes. If the unwillingness to play or desire to invent new rules acts in a non-threatening way then the schism persists as an anomaly about which we care little. If, however, the failure to agree on rules occurs in more severe forms the dominant practice seeks not the compliance of those threatening it but its neutering. Such schisms occur not merely between clashing background conditions of certainty, but within them, and they do so at an overtly political level, at the level of action. Aesthetics, as Plato was well aware, has the capacity to inflame, to transpose, to evoke so public and active a crowd as to warrant censorship in order to maintain the integrity of the ideal state; though less ideal than practical Rorty makes appeal to this creative force and then bridles its use to create a bland politics implausibly smothering the heady bombast and insight of artistic endeavour in a blanket of sympathy.

The move from a question of agreement in vocabulary to an agreement in pain recognition is one from an agreement in opinions, to one in judgements – we have similar relations to the world as language users; but this is not a public–private split for in both inward and outward perspectives we are at risk of collapsing grammatical context into generalized dogma. We are constantly at risk of falling asleep, and being awakened to wonder requires of us a resistance to theories, but it is not the case that it is just theories which hold us certain in our ways. The idea is not that we eliminate dogma by substituting it for a public realm of sympathy, sentimentality, reasonableness and tolerance within which we are able to better explore our private depths, but that we see certainty as a necessary aspect of the life of linguistic selves, but only as an aspect.

PRAGMATISM AND MADNESS

Moving from the elitist aspects of Rorty's liberal politics, through its ethnocentric ones, it is still easily conceivable to see how it retains an alluring sense of integrity. In places it might be a little too pure, but in general the worthy attempt to acknowledge the political as the necessary negotiation of difference, the keen awareness of the paucity of theoretical frameworks in a world viewed linguistically, and the invitation to explore avenues of hope and sentimentality, albeit not compulsory, shows Rorty's politics is very much an expression befitting of a world beset by the critical perspectives of Kant's modern subject. But even here Rorty is confusing in his confidence and surety that despite the contingency of the linguistic perspective *as he conceives it* there are possibilities for correction, improvement and the like.

Invoking Davidson's charity principle where all languages, to the extent that we recognize them as such, are translatable, along with what he identifies as the non-linguistic fact of a common capacity to acknowledge pain, Rorty seems to describe common criteria enabling a minimal (political) mutuality between selves in all but the most extreme of instances. Pragmatic liberals can, then, from within their own culture, seek to translate the languages of other cultures and so widen their sphere of discourse; indeed this is one of the very fence-posts of liberalism: it actively seeks to promote a pluralistic outlook.[38] The increasing sensitization of humanity to ethical principles like the practice of toleration can be seen not as the result of invoking universal dictums more perfectly than before but of the inclusion of ever more human groupings made possible by the increased efficacy of political (public) institutions. In encounters with the extreme where liberal mores cannot accommodate certain pronouncements we may understand others, but we do not have to take their ideas seriously, positive in our own liberal minds that they are just wrong and we are right. Once a certain threshold level is reached, when making appeals to the common stock of truth conditionals present within the nexus of sentences of our own language in order to translate the language of another no longer makes any sense; the charity principle reaches an impasse brought on by the sheer deprivation of the rival perspectives. But is this really an impasse? Are their exhortations so extravagant that, like Descartes meeting those 'whose cerebella are so troubled and clouded by the violent vapours of black bile that they . . . imagine they have an earthenware head or are nothing but pumpkins or are made of glass'[39] all we can do is to treat them as insane? Rorty thinks so.

> We heirs of the enlightenment think of enemies of liberal democracy like Nietzsche or Loyola as, to use Rawls' word, 'mad'. We do so because there is no way of seeing them as fellow citizens of our constitutional democracy, people whose life plans might, given ingenuity and good will, be fitted in with those of other citizens. They are not crazy because they have mistaken the ahistorical nature of human beings. They are crazy because the limits of

sanity are set by what *we* can take seriously. This, in turn, is determined by our upbringing, our historical situation.[40]

The mad are like no-persons in that we can recognize them as physical kin but deny them the linguistic, narrative unity which constitutes their uniqueness as persons – without this thread we can safely see them as not-like-us. Criticism of people can only be mounted from within a language and understanding of their actions can proceed only in so far as we can recognize common truth conditionals. When our historical situation is sufficiently confounded by others as to throw up 'fundamental challenges' to our political world view we respond not with counter-criticism but with the brutality of condescension: we just back away, we send them to cultural Coventry by refusing 'the attack' on our values any offer of a grammatical and hence critical grip. The madness is constituted where persistent irony spills over into political negligence; where the sheer extremity of tangential wanderings give rise to a form of life so overwhelmingly comprehensive as to be incapable of acknowledging the necessity of some form of negotiated public arena. Set firmly on a course for destruction this battleship of fundamentalism[41] is not to be sunk, for that would involve the creation of a theoretical alternative, but avoided. We can hope for its redemption, but we cannot enact or force it.

An initial source of confusion arises over the practice of translation. Rorty conceives it as the establishing of possible coherent interactions within specific contextual practices.[42] This relates to the meaning of words as contrasts with other words grouped in conceptual relations. Speech is not the externalization of the inner mind or a representation of reality but an aspect of subjectivity itself. A radically situated translator or Wittgenstein's explorer[43] translates languages if and only if they are able to establish regular connexions between what people intend and how they act. Thus regularity is the logic of any language and is a product of agreement in forms of life rather than of any synthetic order. In translating the responses of someone as mad, then, we are talking of behaviour which constitutes a complete failure to grasp the point and techniques of a world with regular language: Wittgenstein's 'pupil' who continually opens and shuts a drawer in the hope that what was not there has now actually appeared. But it is clear Rorty is talking of a different kind of madness – a self in possession of a deprived type of language rather than one deprived of language *per se*. To see Nietzscheans, Islamic fundamentalists and even surrealists as insane *because* of their opinions is not tenable; the concept of opinion is not detachable from the conditions of its expression. Having an opinion is to be in a world with language and to be in possession of this language is to be potentially translatable. Rorty's mad are not beyond the bounds of language (and the *Philosophical Investigations* makes clear how strange such a creature would have to be and still resemble a human being) but selves whose depravity can cast our sanity in sharper relief, who re-confirm ourselves to ourselves through bringing home to us the naturalness and familiarity of our concepts and practices.

If this is how words like mad are used then Rorty, despite his indications to the contrary, is not actually ignoring them. By calling them 'mad' he is alluding to a grammatical state of confinement which refuses those so ascribed any critical grip; he is attempting to humiliate them into compulsory re-definition. Turning our backs, feigning indifference and focusing on a myopic betterment is not how we behave when we encounter the alien, the mad; indeed it is because we feel responsible for our values as aspects of our identity and have respect for our own ability to engage in creative language games that we *do* treat threats to such expressive potential seriously – a seriousness we manifest in our urge for grammatical control and containment. To treat the mad like the convicts of the British Empire, beings who we ship into civil non-existence, is not to turn our backs, to ignore, but to create a condition, itself up for narrative description and re-description.

Madness is a criterial ascription rather than a brute datum. As Foucault was acutely aware, the liberal world is often characterized by derision, bound up as it is in the tragedy of suppressing and annihilating the limits of experience found in madness, dreams, sexuality and other arenas of deviance from the confined spaces of disciplined systems of knowledge and science. 'Madness only exists in society; it does not exist outside of the forms of sensibility which isolate it and the forms of repulsion that exclude or capture it.'[44] Under such stratified rubrics concepts like madness and guilt arise not out of difference but the repression of linguistic correctives able to shape the subtleties and nuances of the extreme into monolithic instances of unreason which are to be manipulated and used through processes of enclosure, partitioning, codification and serialization. The confusion of the unknown, the different and the disturbing becomes a hierarchy of knowledge with pre-set rhythms which are absorbed by doctors and patients alike. It is not just in the asylum but in all aspects of what Foucault terms the carceal society that the self becomes dominated by apparatus which organizes our instances of being into stratified compartments each of which has its allotted role. Power is manifest in the teaching of appropriate aptitudes constantly turned in on themselves, discipline being the technique for assuring the Pareto optimal ordering of the multiplicity of all human activities.[45] The self is neither metaphysical constancy nor a fictional creation but a functional unit defined as the space established by lines of control, a useful force defined in accordance with and controlled by established norms. The self is explored and re-described by the strategies (actions upon actions) of a 'machinery of power'.[46] Thus there is no sense to agents moving between the ironical and political, no we-consciousness in contra-distinction to a self-referring contained ironic subject. The rigidity of such a dualism is an adjunct to the machinery being a refined version of an ethics founded on a conception of the self. All we can do is speak from the crenellations of regimes into whatever is in the beyond and in doing so continually re-invent ourselves from within; to confine irony to pure self-government is to miss the stratified impression left on the core of our souls by grammar immersed in power. We are for Foucault as for Wittgenstein selves immersed in forms.

Rorty is disparaging of this post-analytic regime theory, believing Foucault worthy in his Nietzschean sensitivity to the stultifying effects of theoretical addiction, but too pessimistic as to the outcome, forsaking the pragmatic decency of we-consciousness as he does for, as Rorty sees it, an indulgent wallowing in attempts at resisting acculturation and urging upon each self an authenticity and unified purity which it is impossible to achieve. But Foucault's apparatus of power, as with aestheticized forms in general, is not grounded in hopelessness and despair nor in a yearning that autonomy be embedded in public institutions.[47] The former is not a necessary response and the latter not a sensible union. Bentham's panopticon, the 'ideal' apparatus of power, and its totalizing subjectification manifest in each prisoner re-constituting themselves by themselves as model inmates, constitutes a nodal point of domination; igneous power strata are experienced, the prisoner is met with the machinery of perpetual control, *but only because the system turns in on itself*. To achieve equilibrium modes of surveillance and assessment and points of capture inevitably erode themselves because in having to internalize disciplinary modes in order for absolute domination to be achieved selves always experience the possibility of rejection. This is not the inhabitation of a rival system power but an aspect of experience of the ethical action or reflexivity of self on self. The self can never be dominated completely.

Moreover, the concept of power, whilst being pejorative for the liberal, is grammatical for Foucault. Power is the capacity to do or be[48] and so requires in use resistance as much as it does control; power enables as much as it restricts, and so Foucault points to how certain regimes of domination are necessary and beneficial; not everything must embody autonomy, the role of pupil being taught the techniques and purposes of language games being a case in point. Power operates here, but not destructively, for it enables the progression to ethical relations, it opens up the self to the possibility of potential otherness, to facings, the task being to meet disciplinary regimes with new modifications and co-ordinations as well as new forms of politicization by virtue of having been subject to such regimes.

Rorty describes the zealous ironists and fundamentalists as mad, but Foucault shows not only that madness is itself a conceptual ascription which seeks the humiliation of those so conceived, and so shows how Rorty himself is at risk of committing the heinous act of compulsory grammatical re-definition, but that power infuses what we are as selves in its manifold guises. Power as domination risks cruelty, but domination is never total, and power in its fluid forms as action over the actions of others (politics) and action over self (ethics)[49] tells of regimes which are reproducing instantiations of themselves whilst simultaneously provoking the exploration of alternatives. There is much constancy between the regimes talked of by Foucault and grammatical forms of life – experiences of learning, control, direction, myth, bewitchment, efficacy, office and doubt are mutual and it is not tendentious given previous descriptions of self, identity and forms of life to talk of power and teaching as operating in similar ways here. This allusion to similarity between Foucault and Wittgenstein, and it is no more, is illuminating because through an understanding of human forms of life as translatable myth organized as regimes of power it is possible to see how a non-foundationalist ontology of the linguistic self can yield minimal expressions of living embodying aspects of the human experience which whilst not radical as an ideological position taking on all comers has radical implications for politics itself. The linguistic self occupies grammatical spaces which encompass ideas of belief and doubt – indeed it shows the internal connexions between these experiences of learning whereby the mastery of rules can lead either to the rapid internalization and hence stabilization of language games, risking their becoming generalized myth, or to their being taken on and used in novel and contingently obscure ways. Either way prediction on the grounds of certain knowledge – that people are essentially this or that way – makes no sense, nor does principled analysis of which predominates and why; as though if certain measures (institutional) were put in place conditions could be manipulated to make one type predominate over another. The linguistic self is not an absolute type but a description of a particular and its identities which exist in internal relational states as counterparts; a relation permeated by the definitional conditions of grammatical capture which are both used and resisted. If any sense is to be made of the concept of rights amongst such descriptions, it can only come from showing how they might be used as tools of grammatical and artistic power manifest in instances of contextualized resistance, inclusion, amending, effraction, creation and so on. Here human rights would require no metaphysical conceptions of the good nor any justification for their being used; rather they would come to be seen as describing the condition of being in a world with language.

6 Human rights and rules of civility

'What an intelligent man knows is hard to know.' Does Goethe's
contempt for laboratory experiment and his exhortation to us to
go out and learn from untrammelled nature have anything to do
with the idea that a hypothesis (interpreted in the wrong way)
already falsifies the truth? And is it connected with the way I am
now thinking of starting my book – with a description of nature?

(C&V, p. 11e)

So despite its forceful broaching of ordinary language philosophy in
an illuminating foray into political thinking, Rorty's pragmatic
reasoning leaves confused its avowed fidelity to the contingencies of
being, which include the conditionality of the fact of plurality itself.
Given the conception of linguistic self as active rule following creature in a world of possible grammatical regularity manifest in techniques of learning, mastery and stigmatic sanctions such as guilt,
repentance and retribution, the contingencies have a depth not fully
explored by Rorty's hope for a widening appreciation of surface similarities. The linguistic self does not acknowledge other such selves
purely on the basis of public inter-subjective agreement and recognition, but on the habitual, mutual display of imagination, tempera-
ment, will and reflection upon established practices and unrealized
possibilities[1] throughout the many aspects of their lives, both public
and private. This being so, whilst no one good can be identified to
which we are all committed – what is good, in conjunction with
what is right, is determined at least in part within the contextual narrative of a form of life – such a self resonates with a rhythm which
extends beyond that of chance conflations of contingent forces. The
definitional agreement binding such forms of life is not *about* anything and so is not empirical, prudential or ethical. To be about
something would imply that we already occupy positions which

require assessment and reconciliation, ones which themselves would have to be rooted in something else on this type of reasoning. Instead of agreement being the fixing of principles of conduct it is constituted by an *attitude* that we have to others that they have a soul; as distinct from an *opinion* that they are so endowed. Opinions invite response, proof, legitimation, justification whereas an attitude governing a form of life is what enables the possession of opinion in the first place. To embody this attitude to others evokes a sense of self-invocation to constant re-discovery made possible by integration and disintegration and re-integration with what is persistently next to and beyond us. It is to understand and sense what is other as what faces us, distinct, and yet of sense as identities; historically clustered moments of grammatical dignification.

So identity is anthropological; it makes appeal to the possibility of *mutual* receptiveness between prospective, purposive rule followers as members of an evolving community of language use ranging from the unconscious possibilities of myth to the radical effractive and creative exploration of historical limits. Language use is not limited to specific, discrete instances, but takes account of the link between the contextual 'past and now' and the future 'we' that may develop. What cements this use of language is the common attachment we have as beings in a world with language to basic facts of nature, the archaic, though by no means easy to comprehend, aspects of being which feed into the myriad of language games as a kind of primal glue enabling us to move from the basic to the complex, and thence back again. To appreciate these facts is, as Winch says, a primitive recognition of the authority of rules.[2]

So in eschewing theories, foundations and metaphysical ideals the question of beginnings resides with concepts like depth, primitive, pre-rational and basic. Ontology is far from absent in Wittgenstein's work, indeed it is because it is so close to who we are, because it is ever-present, almost mundane, in its persistence that we forgo recognition – being familiar and immediate it is unalluring, it elicits no excitement and goes largely unnoticed. It focuses upon conditions of understanding, action and sense as opposed to foundations of knowledge, contemplation and fact. In this sense where things come to an end for us is not in our seeing things immediately as revelatory or striking, but in our very actions[3] which embody shared pre-linguistic responses and common sensory and learning capacities. These primal facts, however, provide no principles: 'language is not something that is first given a structure and then fitted on to reality';[4]

they have no status as something other than ourselves.[5] Hence: 'Don't take the example of others as your guide, but nature!'.[6]

BASIC FACTS OF NATURE AND CRITERIA

This concept of nature seems to allude to empirical reality but is meant by Wittgenstein to refer to the existence of basic grammatical structures and forms we encounter as pupils of language in which are manifest phenomenal aspects of being. Seeing the importance of primitive language games in dissolving the mental mist in which our everyday use of language is often shrouded[7] Wittgenstein shows how language is built up from basic instances of learning and its extensions. The most basic of such instances are general natural facts which include physiological needs and libidinal strivings along with what Castoriadis refers to as the ensedic logic of living experienced in the possession of such rubrics as basic geometric relations, the ability to distinguish mistakes and produce corrections and a modicum of mutual trust, all of which persist irrespective of specific truth conditionals. There is a sense in which these basic natural facts put the brakes on our speculation as to the sense or criteria, the rules of coherence and continuity,[8] of what it is to be human. They show how it makes sense to conceive of the ability to use grammar as a natural endowment of the whole species,[9] a capacity so familiar in its immediacy and presence that the internally generated authority of its rules manifest as regularity is only apparent in occasional, almost autistic moments of strange absence, where meaning, communication and understanding go in and out of focus as language begins to turn in on itself. It is because of this endowment we can attempt to place ourselves in the position of a radical translator able to describe any other language on the assumption that there always exists enough regularity in ordinary language, the human form of life so to speak. Whilst we are unable to be right or correct in all our actions,[10] whilst we cannot know every application of ordinary language rules, we can exhibit surety whilst being imaginatively open to the possibility of things being otherwise.[11]

So 'to slam the door upon the world' and yet re-open another, to shift our beliefs, to constitute and re-constitute selves in communion with historical and narrative sedimentary layers, requires action which is only made sense of by being in a world with language with established natural facts. The capacity of the linguistic self for expression and association within language games, for attachment to or devolvement from such games and the wider forms of life, for achieving basic levels of security, subsistence, information and consistency, for the use of imperatives, for immersion in conditions, for the grasping of criterial definitions, requires the certainty of myth established not by community alone but by the spontaneous species capacity for regularity expressed in natural facts. Grammatical motion defines the linguistic self not as an essence nor as a construction but as the criterion of identity,[12] the signified object of attention. It is language which lends narrative to our lives, it is through language games that we are able to identify feelings, experiences and actions as our own, and it is grammatical criteria which provide the coherence and continuity to such identity.

Beginning with nature is how Wittgenstein moves beyond both the arbitrariness of an opaque, context-riven being and the absolute certainty of being conceived as empirical reality. It is a nature of basic facts whose presence in a world with language is neither absolute nor arbitrary but manifest in criterial rules of representation; appropriated aspects of the world instances of which resound with the criterial displays determining the meanings of our being in the world. Here representation as aspect seeing requires imagination. Nature as basic facts is to be found in our use of concepts as a kind of schematic outline.[13] They are experienced and so prone to phenomenal accident, but at any historical moment are part of unassailable myths which if doubted foretell the doubt of judgements.[14] This is how they act as criteria: conditions by which ideas are able to get a hold (as in Freud's wish fulfilment)[15] by which coherency in meaning is possible.

Basic facts of nature may be what is required for effective language use, articulating as they do the inherently open, flexible nature of how the linguistic self articulates the weave of identities, but this can only be shown, never legitimated, justified or constructed, either by some form of empirical nominalism or some entirely arbitrary communal signification. The question of ensuring the conditions of effective language use *through proof* is meaningless. They are criteria wrought in the appropriation and re-appropriation of natural, historical and narrative aspects of the world manifest in localized practices and imaginings as those means by which we are able to represent, explain and understand that this or that is the case. Criteria operate as grammatical tethers – they fix the use of concepts (significations), and this fixing of the background conditions of certainty is never absolute, but historically embedded in shifting narrative arrays where facts buck and the river beds change course, meaning the criteria themselves can become contingent and what was once contingent become criteria[16] (what was flowing in the river becomes the river bed and what was once the river bed becomes suspended in the flow).[17] Appropriateness disintegrates, re-integrates and solidifies in course with the established but shifting grammatical techniques of the age; we inhabit its limits which are given not as constructed boundaries but as horizons to perspective.

What counts as criteria is definitional, an historically specific myth, which can change. For example the signification of the concept need changes in line with different stratifications of embedded criteria defining what it is to be a signifier of need. Clearly humans are beings who have a material aspect but from what perspective or direction this aspect is approached depends upon how at any particular moment the rules of the language games and forms of life interlace with the world. The definition of need appears differently in, say, the world view of the Stoic and the hypochondriac, or the Bedouin and the Paladin, or the angel and the donkey. The criterial hues of human rights as a concept arising from the signification of need give testament to this fluidity: where once need was criterially governed by a natural freedom from interference such interference came to have criterial weight as a signified event of necessary basic provision for material subsistence. Similarly, it is imaginable that criteria can again shift; suppose people had multiple personalities and stable identity was inconceivable, hence needs would be split not just across time and place but the discrete space of the signifier; or that animals were defined as possessing needs akin to those of humans. So concepts can be different than they are, it is not at all clear that we know *a priori* which are the simple needs,[18] but they cannot be so different as to suppose their not making sense, their being unimaginable, where the concept has no grip. Though a new concept can be introduced; for example a basic need – an ideal construction distilled as an extreme of the actual from which we can view the actual from a new perspective,[19] the basic need is not an *a priori* absolute but a criterion of humanness – is not a matter of physiology or psychology alone but of being able to see aspects by using limits in whatever ways make sense. Need is not described by the connexion of experience with reality, but a description of *possible* phenomenal experience *as* reality.

FACT AND VALUE

From the perspective of natural facts the move from an 'is' to an 'ought' in ascribing needs and the like becomes otiose; there is no gap to bridge: in this case the fictitious span between people as expressive, creative selves in symbiotic webs of ordinary language use to the universally justified articulation and protection of these selves by virtue of their being committed to and responsible for linguistic expression. To describe an object or a practice is to engage in evaluative judgements as to the usefulness of that practice/object; normative implications in the guise of historically contingent moments of anticipation and aspiration are ensconced in the call for clarity, a call which is never complete but ongoing.[20] If a person is not speaking well, they mumble, hesitate, turn away, guffaw and so on, then not only are they not speaking well, they are not really speaking at all – at least not in accordance with the regularities we have come to accept as the background conditions against which we decide such things; they fail to articulate. In language games we use concepts such as scruffy, good, ugly, inarticulate to convey how we perceive the world – experience cannot be reduced to the perception of objects with names – we experience the world in an imaginative, expressive, always partial and never absolute way.[21] The private language argument shows how the sameness required for the identity of something as fact, or value, is contingent on narrative and performance. How we perform in terms of making sense in any given context is dependent upon how we do in relation to established norms and, so, description, rather than being in conflict with norms, pre-supposes them; we approach and display human dispositions in the Vulgate.

> It seems paradoxical to us that we should make such a medley mixing physical states and states of consciousness up together in a *single* report: 'He suffered great torments and tossed about restlessly.' It is quite usual; so why do we find it paradoxical? Because we want to say that the sentence deals with both tangibles and intangibles at once. – But does it worry you if I say: 'These three struts give the building stability'? Are three and stability tangible? – Look at the sentence as an instrument, and at its sense as its employment.[22]

Language games are played as medleys. Facts and values are not facts and values in isolation but in experience and the empirical nature of any theory is always imbued with conceptual relations.[23]

Invoking natural facts as a human form of life does not require, then, an appeal to a value-based ideal rooted in fact; the distinctions between facts and norms are criterial ones – they appear within narrative flows. Embodied in how we speak with others is the attitude that they have a soul; not that we have satisfied ourselves with the available evidence that they have a soul.[24] This is not a value claim, but a definition best shown by what happens when people are excluded from the linguistic community;[25] when they are refused the status of language use they are refused the capacity to address others by being confined to the status of what Lyotard sees as an ignored 'other'.[26] By this is meant the ordeal of being forgotten identified by Rorty, the imposition of silence upon the language user – as happens in cases of genocide, racism, sexism and the like. Being confined exclusively to the 'other' is that which for those so confined is most unforgettable. There is no greater torment than being lost outside of the swell of grammatical relations, than being a *single* soul. We should not try to cut ourselves off for fear of others looking inside of us. We can be ashamed of what we are, but to be ashamed of ourselves before others and so seek to hide away is to perpetuate the torture of feeling lost or to smother our partiality with an overt concern for surface appearances.[27] In order to understand this people should be prepared to acknowledge that the dynamics of grammar allows for perspectives to change or even for a change in natural facts.[28] This incorporates an aspect of translation which is less its possibility than the responsibility attendant on its being imaginatively possible in all instances of human interaction. To attend to Lyotard's 'other' is to acknowledge it as what faces us. This facing is not a fact in a static state of nature nor an embodiment of definite principle but a dynamic anticipation of communion with other perspectives. 'Attention consists in preparedness to follow each smallest movement that may appear.'[29] Thus, language must always reveal the potential of the 'other', including showing those other than ourselves as selves, and this understanding of the self cannot take place without the whole environment of such an event of understanding, a multitude of circumstances.[30]

This is not a case of re-enchanting[31] the ontological condition of selves, but to show how it is selves come to display identities in a world with language by processes of immersion, effraction and creation. These activities are not solely ironic and hence insulated and introspective. For the self to even contemplate alternatives they must be part of the stage setting of digested and secreted orthodox opinions. Using the old languages as a base from which to test the limits, to let off the brakes and explore, involves a grasp of technique and an employment of imagination which requires first and foremost what Wittgenstein sees as activity and will 'in overcoming opposing forces and frictional resistances'; activity and will whose effort 'does not show in the distance he travels but perhaps only in the heat he generates in overcoming friction'.[32] In going back to the rough ground in order to make sense of belonging, practising, participating and contributing we also have to countenance frictional resistance, and this resistance occurs throughout narratives. Our contingencies cannot be negotiated away as such, even temporarily for the cause of public solidarity; the facing is always present as that which we encounter when looking to switch from one perspective to another, to slam one door and open another. That this is neither fact nor value but criteria suggests it is possible to envisage describing a practice which all humans potentially share and from which it makes sense to invoke acknowledgements of the attitude we have to others as selves in possession of a soul. It is this concept of practice, or field of activity and will, as defined through sense, and not truth, which makes possible any talk of human-wide criteria, of what Michael Oakeshott terms the postulates of human conduct.[33]

CRITERIA AND POSTULATES

To understand the facts of living as facts in such a dissolute *mélange* of attraction and effraction involves a shift from the identification, explanation and justification of the characteristic elements of human conduct conceived in some form of causally explicative line of discrete events to an identification of the 'goings on' in the world, a shifting array of non-reducible and non-linear activities, in terms of their conditions, or the postulates which render them intelligible.[34] To understand relations found in human conduct *in toto* requires us to postulate the concept practice: a 'set of considerations, manners, uses, observances, customs, standards, canons, maxims, principles, rules and offices specifying useful procedures or denoting obligations or duties which relate to human actions and utterances'.[35] So a practice is a set of understood conditions or considerations subscribed to by selves which guide the form and content of action adverbially: we behave rightfully, inaccurately, sensibly, weirdly and so on. As criteria of human conduct they are plastic; though potentially hardened as institutional mores no practice is 'immune to modifications incidentally imposed upon it by the performances it qualifies'.[36] Oakeshott conceives of practices as a kind of sediment left by the flow of performance or conduct, continuously unfinished, which postulate the relations of agents engaged in the performances from which they arise or in which they are designed.

Oakeshott, like Wittgenstein, is evoking/imagining the role which such practices have in our lives – imagine our relation to a practice and we can imagine different relations conceived with different types of limiting cases, what it must have been like or will be like to follow different signposts. Oakeshott is describing what Wittgenstein termed a kind of 'musical' sensitivity to variations on themes – you see it in this key, conceive that bar as an opening, it must be phrased like this. By noticing aspects, new perceptions coupled with old ones, we are moving amongst instances of *accepting* different language games – such that when we encounter an image, say of three intersecting lines, we say things of the order: that is a geometric shape; that is a dunce's hat; that is a symbol for a mountain; that is a mediæval symbol for melancholy; that is a piece of neo-plastic art; and so on. These images force themselves upon us as concepts; we have *attitudes* towards them which vary, and it is in revealing these different attitudes that aspects dawn upon us, and then we see them as this, or that. *Now* it is a geometric shape, *now* a mediæval symbol and so on.[37]

In moving from the identification, explanation and justification of characteristics to a description of postulates we can never be aware of the full depth of an image, a concept or an action; only of significant contexts which shift the impression we have of things. In witnessing the dawning of an aspect we are not witnessing the inherent properties or characteristics of an object, but internal relations between it and other things. This is what is meant by Wittgenstein in seeing things as a *state* of imagination and will internally linked to perception; 'I am seeing leaf green', 'I am seeing a triangle', for each time we are interpreting things, thinking, doing something, *but not in advance* – we learn what it is to have a state of seeing through our immersion in the conditionalities governing this or that aspect of seeing.[38] 'Seeing an aspect and imagining are subject to the will. There is such an order as "Imagine *this*", and also: "Now see the figure like *this*"; but not: "Now see this leaf green".'[39] We are looking at how the concept of green is used, under what aspects it arises, and not determining its existence. Postulates describe how in this context we make this utterance; and it is only from within this context of utterance, or language game, that we can speak of thought, will, intending, etc. In finding the right word, in the dawning of an aspect, in saying: 'now I know how to go on', we are not looking inside of us to see what is going on; it is an expression we use in specific circumstances where we have become certain, where the postulates become arenas of conditional possibility. Willing, interpreting aspects, requires expectations embedded in situations from which they take their rise. Human will, therefore, cannot stop short of action itself.[40] To understand the human will, then, is to understand instances of human conduct; the future realization of an expectation is not an event distinct from that expectation, and such understanding is not to find the real, exact, inner meaning of words as though there were some causal relation between the world of meaning and that of expression, but to show how our acting, our creativity, is found through postulates, conditional fields of expression and aspect vision.

Human conduct is conceived as some form of grammatically appropriate self-disclosure cast in terms of self-understandings and misunderstanding. This is not a subjective inner process of goal-orientated effort, for these are not *my* understandings as such, but my *understandings*; instances of grammatical understanding which can be investigated. Nor is it understanding at a general level, for they remain specific understandings – I want, for instance, an agonal public life, or a packet of peanut M&Ms, or the right to be free from torture, each of which require that we postulate certain conditions – the process of deliberation and argument, having a sweet tooth or the influence of product imaging, the concept of right – and decide what constitutes an instance in each case. I cannot *want*, however, happiness in general, for that admits of no postulate, no condition; to want for happiness requires no postulate other than that of conduct itself.

When investigating the many instances of these postulates, and in doing so constantly meeting with new understandings waiting to be understood, we must not, warns Oakeshott, confuse the postulates of conduct with grand principles, superior and absolute substitutes for existing understandings from which we are to elicit 'correct' performances.[41] Postulates are necessarily limited by conditionality and, often, by our being unaware of such conditionality; they are the limits to forms of life towards which we can construe understanding whilst being aware of the hegemonic tendency to collapse them into dogma. To wish for the ultimate legitimating postulate is nonsensical; to eternally substantiate the substantial is to have language idling. Oakeshott and Wittgenstein are both at pains to show there is no ideal ordering of the self for reasoning to grasp and orientate itself towards, no complete understanding of all possible instances of will, be it a supreme rational being or merely one phenomenological instance amongst a totality of facts. The mistake goes something like this: either the will is free by virtue of its primacy to and independence from the realm of changeable experience which it some-how uses in order to further furnish its iridescent insubstantiality, or it is determined by a choice set which amounts to little more than the tightening and loosening of screws of a phenomenological machine whose configuration and purpose it cannot fathom or change. The former is self as demiurge, the latter self as fashion victim – both are symptoms of a linguistic delusion which views will as predicated by some form of Pareto optimal reasoning on behalf of noumena or structure. The result is either total causal freedom or total causal determinism, or some mushy compatibilist agglomeration of the two. Our addiction to psycho-physical parallelism encourages us to explain instances of will as consequential progressions in an algorithmic chain (of the sort purpose formation, means formation, action, achievement) resulting in a specific human type.

RATIONAL POLITICS

A passion for specific human types, theories and ideals expressed in the longing for immutable postulates tends to the view that social relations are the outcome of a specific cause: for example the socio-logical (class system), psychological (ego functioning), rational (supreme law, absolute interest) or biological (selfish gene). What Wittgenstein and Oakeshott show is that the self is not to be con-ceived in foundational terms of reality or convention at all, and agency is to be seen as neither voluntary nor non-voluntary. To act is a grammatical event internally linked by instances of persistent conscious understanding regulated by practices which we approach through description and definition. The linguistic self has a narrative, a story of belonging to and moving beyond fields of conditionality, or language games, whereby it deliberates and chooses through its own responses to understood scenarios. To cultivate the spaces, gaps and facings in the forms of language use without resenting or regretting such contingency, whilst being able to assess and adjust such culti-vation in the light of opaque futures and divergent responses to tradition, is to conceive of a person content and disposed to act from within their intelligent resources of self-enactment (authenticity) and self-disclosure (use).[42]

Oakeshott and Wittgenstein both display an active hostility to theoretical constructions of reason because of their generalist aspira-tions; and to reduce civic motion specifically to the model of a rational plan, a constructed contract, an absolute system of relations or a revealed principle is to reduce the authenticity of living to an anodyne level of conformist constructivism: a behaviour *deliberately* directed to the achievement of a *formulated* purpose and governed solely by that purpose. Here the civic condition becomes the political upshot of a sovereign self – the progenitor of all action or some Baconian child bathed in amniotic innocence who gradually acquires knowledge and understanding as it goes to meet the world of forces, laws and constraints. Either way the *consequent* job of politics becomes the provision of optimal conditions for the full articulation of this deliberate, self-generated activity devoid of the polluting effects of mystery, fluidity, habit, tradition and other atmospheric annoyances,[43] something which is legitimated by reference to such a self.

The politics consequent upon human rights promotes the sanctity of self-consciousness and principle (the feeling the self has for the self as the only thing it is really possible to feel for) as set intractably against that of structure. The neo-Kantian liberal narrative with its equation of certitude with an absence of prejudice, a passion for observable stability and an eschewal of elites portrays the political as the institutional protection of self from self. Preoccupied with the creation of functional, detailed, uniform conditions created by bringing to account before the individual will all institutions of control[44] this rationalist politics assumes it escapes bias by constantly pandering to the isolate mind. But this coupling of reasonableness and reason in a thin theory of the good risks re-directing our attention away from the very real responsibilities, inconsistencies and pragmatic immediacy of living amongst fluid linguistic boundaries. Considering rational solutions perfect ones, rationalist politics considers itself a system for all seasons and comes to perceive those activities which fail to fall in line with its plans, with its doctrines and its impulse, as the cumbersome and obscuring ruminations of some genetically inbred, backwater folk-mentality whose time is surely but a few moments from entering totemistic oblivion. The rules of rationalist politics aspire to universalize – certain in their technique they attempt to impose a specific substantive goal, a blueprint for social rejuvenation expressed in writing by lists of principles imbued with the beatific glow of some 'golden dawn'.

The Enlightenment, the historical moments Oakeshott identifies as constituting the genesis of this rationalist perspective, witnessed a revolutionary shift in our faith from a proselytizing Christianity to an equally vehemently dogmatic condition of rational exclusionism – all that matters being the achievement of rationally (eschatologically) formulated progress. For Oakeshott our self-incurred immaturity (nonage) persisted; only the shackles shifted from a spiritual to a temporal set of *a priori* absolutes. From this period onwards politics has been prone to becoming a central production process of the satisfaction for felt need. These felt needs are less informed by concrete knowledge of social interests than by the abstract rules of books, a *saeculum rationalisticum*,[45] which mistakenly conceives of traditions, practices, habits as restricting of the true self. We are to live in accordance with projects and codes which are somehow lain over our day-to-day lives like some mesh in order that events of a disturbed and dissolute order have little chance of arising.

What the ensuing political projects ignore is that much of what we do when we follow the rules resists strict formulation, control and rigour – to have power is to pre-suppose the possibility of things being other than they are. Much of our activity is nuanced, intimate, subtle, emerging, and can be grasped only through a homeopathic sensitivity to what Oakeshott refers to as the ongoing intimations[46] of human conduct: the knowhow appropriate in any language game given our training, tradition and aims. This knowhow is never so formulated as to be absolute – exceptions, amendments, alterations and shifts in emphasis are always a possibility, though these need not bring the force of the rule out of focus; it's just that the brakes are being applied, the limits being posited, at different periods of the language game. Oakeshott sees rationalism as perfecting what he terms technical knowledge, the universally applicable codes and principles of the social scientists, to the exclusion of practical knowledge, conceived idiosyncratically by Oakeshott as conduct in respect of the acknowledgement of practices learnt through intimation, familiarity, apprenticeship, tradition, unspoken connoiseurship, hints, gestures, use and so on.[47] Thus, full understanding becomes a 'faithfulness to the knowledge we have of how to conduct the specific activity we are engaged in',[48] a faithfulness requiring self-understanding through education, familiarity and use.

Such faith, however, is not blind. Acting from within a language game or form of life does not mean we are prisoners, destined to live out our days cognizant of nothing other than the shadowy illusions cast by the fires burning in our own specific cave. The linguistic self uses rules which describe norms of conduct; they articulate those conditions it is proper to subscribe to when following a language game, a composition of identified and described conditions of conduct which can only subsist in being understood and recognized as 'the way to go' in this instance. There is always a pattern to human activity but this pattern is not superimposed, it is inherent in the activity itself.[49] They make no claim to be obeyed or be expressly enacted, nor to any jurisdiction over actions performed prior to their being followed. In Oakeshott's words 'Rules assert norms of conduct, they do not determine or forecast what will be said or done'.[50] They do not make choices by controlling the will of the rule follower, but show what decisions have to be taken should it be sensibly said that the rule is being followed.

It is the self-authenticating, self-adjudicating nature of rules which rationalist politics fails to distinguish from the substantive aspect of rule following. Whilst rules can be theorized about in terms of their conditions, whilst their use can be approved or disapproved of, whilst they can be imperative or confer power, and whilst they can be used to justify positions in argument, they enjoin, justify, prohibit or warrant conditions to subscribe to which does not collapse into an approval of specific substantive actions and purposes. Rationalist politics conflates these aspects of rule following and so tumbles swiftly into the mire whence it tries vainly to seek bedrock in the guise of absolute, substantive principles such as those designed to acknowledge and institute autonomous will. Oakeshott sees politics as doomed lest it eschew the ideas either of managing policy towards some desired aim or the enjoining of a common purpose and in its stead focus exclusively on thinking and speaking about the desirability of the conditions prescribed by those rules of civil intercourse to which we assent as citizens.[51]

CIVIL ASSOCIATION

Whilst human conduct can be conceived in terms of propositions these propositions can in no sensible way be the cause of such conduct, for there is no way to determine a purpose or means towards it in advance of the conduct itself. Self-understanding cannot be acquired independently of conduct, indeed to talk of such knowledge requires the conceptual stage setting of already established practices in which the self acts. If, then, it is in accordance with rules, and more generally a practice composed of rules, that the human conduct postulated by practice is to be conceived, then in what sense can these conditions be said to be political; how are the relations governed by rules to be negotiated, instituted, challenged and repealed? Oakeshott re-configures this investigation by conceptualizing these relations as those of civility. To understand civility for Oakeshott is to acknowledge *cives* or citizens as beings who are related solely in terms of a common recognition of those rules which constitute the practice of civility. The only way these conditions resonate in all human conduct is if they are the described conditions to be acknowledged by all *cives* in all cases. Oakeshott renders such a condition explicit in his distinction between the practice of enterprise aimed at the realization of a voluntarily aspired to specific state of affairs where the conditions or postulates are informed by the purposive and substantive aims of the practice, and non-optional civic practices whose rules refer not to purpose but the enactment, clarification and adjudication of civilly desirable rules.

On this reading civility itself becomes an idiom, a practice, but one which is akin neither to a specific game nor to what Oakeshott terms an enterprise association (it has no specific set of wants it sets out to realize) – the association begins and ends in the recognition of rules of common responsibility. It is, then, a peculiarly general type of practice or language game, one whose rules not only describe and prescribe specific conditions in a clear and non-arbitrary manner, but do so contingently and formally rather than incidentally. A civic association or *civitas* becomes a self-sufficient relationship of selves linked solely in terms of the practice of civility in which the conditions of the practice are not used up in their being used. The relations are ongoing; the rules are grasped, mastered and used in countless ways. Rules do not require specific actions by means of force, but by means of the internally generated conditions of description brought about historically as being that which we do.

This ambience of this civil society is captured by rules from which the capacity for ruling flows, these Oakeshott calls *lex*;[52] they do not coerce,[53] but act as conditioning limits whose jurisdiction is continuously explored and reconstituted in a non-exclusive and formal enactment of explored formal relations engaged with the adverbial terms upon which satisfactions can be sought, and not with the satisfactions themselves. The system of rules acknowledged by *cives* Oakeshott calls *respublica* – the considerations of *cives* both in a system of rules and in common recognition of such rules as rules.[54] These considerations partake of a formality which only becomes fully understood by virtue of an associated, though not strictly formal, political engagement with the consequences of certain conditions.[55] Firstly, a legislative concern for the enactment and repeal of rules in order that the system remain flexible in the face of historical contingency. Secondly, the need for ruling which assents to and asserts *respublica* in enacted conditions which the civil society expects to persist.[56] Lastly comes the need for adjudication – the assessment of conflicting or improperly or imperfectly applied rules. These elements of praxis enable the considerations of *cives* to have force, but form no part of civil association. Politics acts like a conduit between this ideal, abstracted acknowledgement of rules and their praxis. It is the deliberation of *respublica* in terms of the desirability of condition; a substantive concern which nevertheless remains inextricably linked with the civil condition by virtue of its focus on condition rather than policy.[57] Politics becomes a concern for the sustenance of civility, an ongoing attention to the clarity of the conditions as opposed to the objectives of our internally generated obligations.[58]

The resultant civil condition would exclude from the political, according to Oakeshott, as showing a substantive concern with specific purposes as opposed to the possibility of purpose, such institutions as *bills* of rights, free markets, the police, civil servants, social workers, national anthems, democracy and a myriad of other such enterprises. These can form fit topics for debate, but in no way define the conditions of civil association where what is required is an internally generated obligation to comply with *lex* along with a subscription to procedures for enacting, amending and changing it. Any change must be effected and judged in accordance with conditions of civic activity, and with no concern for the effects of such activity. The authority of the civil condition goes unexamined; deliberation is concerned with specific instances of the civil mode, outside of which there exist no criteria for any possible political deliberation. To concern oneself with civil praxis is already to invoke the authority of the rules whose implementation one is considering.

Likened by Oakeshott to sailing directionless on a sea with no shore for shelter and no bed for anchorage the civil condition, on first encounter, seems at best tautological and at worst a convoluted re-conceptualization of the private language from where procedure, form and continuity breath their own homogenized air, have no substantive reliance and exist irrespective of power, control, reason, will and understanding. If by the rules of civil association Oakeshott is claiming to have accessed a form of authority which is capable of generating its own conditions of regularity (authority, power), a configuration of purely formal civil form running *sui generis* to actual conditions of living, then the resultant interdicts would be so rarefied and hollow as to be the inconsequential upshot of an entirely facile exercise of perfect internal confirmation – a kind of dreamboat Bilbo Baggins journey on which the citizen is taken further and further away from empirical instances and towards the clarification and hence eradication of sublimity. In so focusing his attention

Oakeshott is forgetting, says Flathman, that following a rule adverb-ally, whilst it requires no explicit substantive aim, still requires textual purpose. To behave recklessly, civilly, despondently only makes sense given the possibility of being reckless, civil and despondent. Flath-man sees the civil condition being so pure in its exactness and correct-ness that it is abstracted from historical accident and context to a state of meaningless form. That in his urge to abate contingency in rule following, to seek a scenario of perfectly understood conditions, Oakeshott forgets that civil association requires a lot of prior stage setting, that it is inherently contestable in terms of its own criteria of assessment.[59]

That Oakeshott was avowedly hostile to such esoteric musings on the absolute, that he wished by understanding the goings on of the world 'to abate mystery rather than to achieve a suppositious definit-ive understanding',[60] suggests, however, a political mind very much concerned with an historical and conditional story of civil living. His writings are peppered with allusions to historical circumstances, nar-rative conditions and partial understandings; indeed it is the acute awareness of what he sees as the ongoing intimations of human conduct that leads him into a consideration of that aspect of social living he calls civil association, accessed via the description of *respublica* as distinct from enterprise, which has a possible sense as requiring internally legitimated authority. Flathman sees Oakeshott as equating this authority with the surrender or suspension of judge-ment, whereby the prospective citizen exercises extreme self-discipline in showing no concern for values and interests, concentrating exclu-sively on the conditions of deliberation.[61] For Flathman such con-siderations always require judgement, whereby agents as citizens acknowledge that in a certain context a certain rule should be fol-lowed without question *because of* their being in a specific relational and hence reflective and judgemental position.[62] In insisting that those who would be ruled, the citizens, embrace an exclusive concern with *respublica*, Oakeshott is painting an impossibly pure form.

But Oakeshott's concern is not with construction nor the erection of limiting boundaries with the express purpose of blinkering per-spectives on rule to the civic, with creating a split between the public and the private whereby at certain moments (being obedient) we focus exclusively on being a citizen. Private and public are not differ-ent components of citizens, actions or places (the *agora* is not the physical marketplace) but relations which meet 'in every substantive engagement'.[63] *Respublica,* being that aspect of our conduct con-cerned with conditions of substance, avoids residing in either space, for it is not delineating a specific space, but conveying the sensible and ongoing conception of relational spaces themselves constituted in a 'diurnal intercourse' which organizes contingent modes of understanding by virtue of its internally generated authority. Conceiving these *cives* as linguistic selves shows how this self-understanding is possible. To be a language user, to feel a grammatical commonality in regularity, relates those who otherwise would not be related by virtue of self-authenticating language use. They create and delineate a civic being whose coherence is totally dependent upon the symmetry of the relationship between the language games themselves, by virtue of which they continuously interrupt and accommodate one another.

The authority of these rules is not separate from the everyday action of rule following beings, but internal to it. Flathman seems to be invoking the need to appeal to community agreement as the final court of appeal as to how we are to go in following a rule. We follow by virtue of our judging in accordance with some evaluative criteria or other that this is in fact the correct way to go. But as Wittgenstein shows, in behaving regularly we are not following rules with the aid of external checks or judgements; we do not turn around and check our performance, we just follow, and it seems that Oakeshott is aspiring to convey a similar description in his delineation of civil association. *From a certain perspective* it is possible to conceive of rule following as having internally generated criteria of regularity, for that is simply part of being in a world with language, and moreover, this aspect forms part of what it is to live socially. It is an aspect of our practices imbued with historical purpose and myth that they generate their own terms and conditions from which it is possible to envisage, nevertheless, a switch. Thus the rules of civil association do not invoke approval or judgement; they require assent, or dissent, or indifference, each of which is a possible (intelligible) relation to adopt. Oakeshott was very alive to the possibility of failing in one's civil obligation, but this failure is not a misunderstanding, it is an identification of a practice of which the self is not a part. If a self refused to be civil on grounds that it somehow failed to reflect what was crucial about themselves – it failed to fully realize their wishes, or create a sphere of fully rational autonomy for all, or provoked bad consequences, it would be failing to understand what the rule is for, believing it to aspire to specific substantive aims rather than the definition of conditions. Oakeshott is not forcing the citizen to take cognizance of a single aspect to the exclusion of all others, forcing us somehow to suppress our musical sensitivity, to constantly see just one thing (which would be as weird as forcing us to witness only a single aspect, the triangle as geometric shape and not as neo-plastic art, for instance) but to show how descriptions of the world rest on definitions whose temporally and historically instituted authority is required as a postulate to any understanding of those descriptions. On encountering the dawning of an aspect where now this is seen, now that, we do not stand in a relation of interpretation or judgement, but one of acknowledgement and assent which dawns over us, and can just as soon cloud over, or switch to another. It is in giving witness to this ebb and flow that Wittgenstein shows how it is sensible to conceive of a self construed linguistically, as a being for whom will is an ongoing solidification and erosion of grammatical positions; and it is in exploring the political ramifications of this self devoid of foundations, substantive aims, ultimate guiding principles, that Oakeshott conceives of the importance of conversation in the civil condition.

THE CONVERSATION AND THE GRAMMATICAL

With regard to citizens what has to be postulated is a moral condition of *respublica* with its political conduit of praxis in order that we may make sense of an aspect of social living, the civil condition, whose authority is immanent in grammatical history, as opposed to empirical. Civic rules are suggestive of an association emerging through an acknowledgement of the conditions of grammatical relations; a recognition of rules as rules *per se* which requires no external threat of sanction or reward of commendation in order to have force. The force or authority stems from what it is to go by a linguistic practice, irrespective of the substantive aim of any specific practice. The rules of this condition seek not to persuade, refute or inform but to articulate what Oakeshott calls the conversation of mankind in which there is no enquiry for truth nor conclusions reached, no information provided nor succour sought, no argument dismissed nor possibility excluded.

In conversation, 'facts' appear only to be resolved once more into the possibilities from which they were made; certainties are shown to be combustible, not by being brought into contact with other 'certainties' or with doubt, but by being kindled by the presence of ideas of another order; approximations are revealed between notions normally remote from one another. Thoughts of different species take wing and play around with one another, responding to each others' movements and provoking one another to fresh exertions. Nobody asks where they have come from or on what authority they are present; nobody cares what will become of them when they have played their part. There is no symposiarch or arbiter; not even a doorkeeper to examine credentials. Every entrant is taken at its face-value and everything is permitted which can get itself accepted into the flow of speculation . . . Properly speaking, it is impossible in the absence of a diversity of voices: in it different universes of discourse meet, acknowledge each other and enjoy an oblique relationship which neither requires nor forecasts their being assimilated to one another.[64]

The practice of civility, unlike that of rationalist politics, does not seek to accumulate information about ourselves and our world, nor is it some form of Habermassian or even Rortyan process of inter-subjective exclusively public agreement, but a continuous enactment and re-enactment of a civic vernacular in which language users, or agents, recognize and disclose themselves as *cives* and where *cives* acknowledge and continuously explore their relation with one another – 'It is a language which both contains and responds to the imaginative inventions of *cives*'[65] which take flight in the many and varied language games, idioms and practices present in human conduct.

Oakeshott's civility yields the basic experience of being in a world with language – a persistent, unrehearsed imaginative adventure of belonging, losing, re-generating and creating during which we come to learn to recognize the innumerable voices or practices of human conduct, to discern proper utterances, to learn and reject habits. The tendency in such conversation is for voices to capture rigidified agglomerations of *knowledge*, or for them to exhibit bad manners through *superbia* and seek to display an exclusive concern with one's own utterances and hence identify the conversation with the self. Civility consists, then, in each voice having the impetus for serious engagement whilst resisting any undue solidity of perspective. We have to be alive to the differences between things. The point is not to exclude the current political concerns with plans, principles and the like, but to resist their collapse into being the only idioms of legit-imate expression, to show how an aspect of social living, and a crucial one for the concepts of authority, power and right, involves the consideration of conditions of rule following on their own terms. To desire a monolithic perspective on this medley is not only to exclude other voices, but to conceive of such exclusion as desirable, resulting in a monotonous politics of one-dimensional agendas or ideologies in which one seeks the annihilation of the other.

By conceiving of the human self as something manifest in instances of action, an imagining being capable of making, recognizing and moving about images in manners appropriate to their character (the considerabilities demanded by technique or skill), and not as some antecedent receptacle or generic core, Oakeshott wants to open up an idea of civility characterized by the confluence of various language games, or idioms of imagining, measured not by reference to some central ideal but specified in relation to how they distinguish from and relate to other such idioms. Thus whilst ideological or realist discourse urging the discovery of truth, or practical discourse urging the realization of the pragmatic, or the poetic discourse urging us to the plane of the contemplative muse, partake of the conversation of mankind, none ought dominate. There is no one right way to do or be save for the freeing up of institutions in order to permit the maximal extent of civility; a civic space within which people come to develop the habit of self-articulation and self-enclosure through engagement in language games.

> It is the ability to participate in this conversation, and not the ability to reason cogently, to make discoveries about the world, or to contrive a better world, which distinguishes the human from the animal and the civilized man from the barbarian.[66]

The limits are intrinsic limits of coherence whereby language in its historical, narrative, psychological and natural guises is made sensible.

BASIC FACTS, HUMAN RIGHTS AND MORAL CONDITIONS

In its anxiety to eschew substantive, prudential aims the impressions left by Oakeshott's civil condition are like momentary visions, mirages amongst the vernacular which are created and reflected upon by the citizen as propriety relations in the dissonance of human conduct, as graceful sentiments infusing activity, but which remain distant, alluring intimations. Oakeshott sees morality as an ongoing aesthetic of self-enactment in the face of 'evanescence and mutability'.[67] The relations described herein evoke a spirit of the fugitive adventurer exploring substantively unresolved and inconclusive states using such sentiments as courage, honour, integrity, devilry, malice and other such Machiavellian mores; the conditions in which the aims and purposes in human conduct are sought in the ongoing journey of self-enactment and self-disclosure; the self becomes less a generic unity than a dramatic identity.[68] Proceeding artistically (a practice having both the aspect of a mastered art and a procedure relating would-be artists[69]), and devoid of models of perfection and in possession of attitudes or dispositions towards things, morality is a conditioned exploration of conditions; conditioned neither by substantive fact nor by mankind, but by a continual encounter with adepts, practitioners, quacks, charlatans, pupils and teachers in relations of 'reflective consciousness, understanding, deliberation',[70] which are the conditions of all human goings-on.

These postulates are not reductions from actual states of affairs, be they instances of specific actions or specific social belief patterns, but ones wrought and re-wrought in the steady realization that to understand the concept of self is to *show aspects* of self-enactment; it is not to prove, to give examples of or to justify them. It is in this sense that to follow a rule is to accept the intelligibility of doing this, or that, and not to be controlled, or coerced into this or that (and hence present reasons for doing this or that).[71] This condition of acknowledging those conditions to be subscribed to should one be said to be playing this or that language game shows how human rights can be intelligible as rules. They do not coerce or prescript (that they can be used in this way is a confusion resulting from a lack of rigour in separating 'enterprise' from 'civil') but articulate the condition of being in a world with language. They are considerations to subscribe to in the practices of self-disclosure and self-enactment; the 'art of agency'.[72] They are inextricably linked to activity as rules not to be appealed to as legitimating but as enabling by virtue of their having been learnt, understood and used. They provide us with the means by which we come to decide upon the intelligibility and sense of actions, not their final purpose. Here human rights practice requires a mastery of technique and style, a mastery which is learnt as a language; we grasp the rules, individuated through aesthetic style, and by taking them we are able to say 'now I can go on'. The moral limits articulated by human rights show the historical medley of conditions to be subscribed to if living is to be creative and not imitative – to postulate limits is not to say what you are putting them there for; the limits define, they do not proscribe such that they show how to do what we do and not what to do in any sense.

So self-recognition arises through relations between human actions and utterances understood in terms of the multiplicity of connexions with other such actions and utterances; connexions made as family resemblances. These relations are contingent, they touch in terms of their belonging together 'as composing an intelligible continuity of conditionally dependent occurrences'.[73] This continuity of action and utterance occurs as a continuous invocation where the antecedent is seen neither as progenitor nor as a discrete moment in teleological progression but as activity calling for response, and the consequent is seen as acknowledgement. Thus 'The continuity is not merely absence of interval: it is the congruity of what came after with what went before'.[74] So understanding of self requires both the positing of conditions and the narrative and historical identification of instances of those positions. To understand is to ask in what sort of contexts do such actions and utterances occur,[75] contexts which far from being hermetically sealed off from each other, constitute mutual conditions of intelligibility as aspects of the ongoing conversation.

So the conversation alludes not to a proof, but a conditional description of what it is to be a self, one akin to the form of linguistic self arising from grammatical considerations of human agency. The converse is to conceive of the world contingently; it is the criterion of morality. That language use as conversation evokes the spirit of the self as an expectant adventurer shows how an awareness of the historicity of being, the immersion of self in language and contingency, does not require of us as moral beings some sceptical reliance on prudential conditions of stability, some tale of the absolute beginning or end, or some sentimental appeal to the possibility of pain, but a continuous conditional embrace of the conditions of conversation internally linked to specific instances of such conversation. If human rights were acknowledged as being expression of such an embrace, their being invoked not as principles with aim but rules requiring assent if the continuity of conversation is to persist, then such requirements as they pose become intelligible to those embodying the basic natural facts of language use, irrespective of any substantive end to which that embodiment is put.

This cannot be proved, but shown, through the admission of imaginative alternatives to such basic natural facts of language use and their bewildering, almost alien presence, which serves to set in greater relief the naturalness of concepts like human rights when conceived of as postulates to the civil condition. We describe our nature by imagining what is beyond. To envisage a society devoid of the postulates of civility, devoid of conversation, is to give witness to beings for whom politics is at best a temporary annoyance to be transcended, one which seeks universal stability and contentment, one in which problems are absent and principles absolute, one where negotiation is replaced by revealed embodiment and intonations of conversation suffused under the constant drone of arrived-at equilibrium. Reflecting upon what such a society would be serves to remind us of how we just are beings immersed in the effractive, creative, belonging, disciplined and explorative aspects of language use. So human rights evoke the bonds of language use expressed through continually evolving relational expressions held in place by the centripetal force of mutual enclosure and disclosure from within practices, be they established, decaying or nascent, rather than something which controls them. There is no sense of substantive right or wrong. There is an

> absence of a victor [which] help[s] articulate the fact that in a democracy embodying good enough justice, the conversation over how good its justice is, must take place and also must not have a victor, that this is not because agreement can or should always be reached, but because disagreement, and separateness of position, is to be allowed its satisfactions, reached and expressed in particular ways.[76]

Cives cannot exempt themselves from human rights so described, for as rules they are the very condition of civility, but they can violate them, and to resist the temptations of violation requires a vicious coolheadedness, an acknowledgement that the postulates of civility require a constant willing to face the perpetual presence of the other, the tragedy, sublimity and potentiality of the facing. We arrive at 'a temple providing a setting for the passions without meddling with them',[77] one which seeks not to allay our fears or fully negate our problems but to clarify our relations, to make our activity apparent and render what is human to what it makes sense to say.

Notes

INTRODUCTION: WHY WITTGENSTEIN

1 Onora O'Neill 'Transnational Justice' in David Held (ed.) *Political Theory Today*, Polity Press, 1991, pp.276–304.

2 Jack Donnelley *Universal Human Rights*, Cornell University Press, 1989, Chs 3, 6, talks of how burgeoning trade governed through the bureaucratic mechanisms of organizations like GATT and the World Bank is implanting a truly universal, homogenized view of life upon everyone. Human rights respond to the need to preserve human dignity in the face of collapsing traditional group-based identities, they provide a home for people's self-identity, securing it against possible disorientation in an increasingly electrified world. Similar overtures to the spread of *homo oeconomicus* are made by those who see the collapsing of 'communist states' and rapid development in the Pacific Rim as indicative of the efficacy and health of the free market way of doing things.

3 Human rights are becoming understood in direct proportion to the spread of market relations and the quanta used for assessing conditions consequent upon such relations. So, for example, UNESCO measures poverty as a per capita figure; foreign aid is given as moneys or loans tied into trade contracts; and the 'freeing up' of China is seen as the gradual emergence of a vast new market and not as the shedding of political or spiritual bondage.

4 Though for Locke (*Two Treatises on Government* (1689), Routledge, 1903) the chief aim of government was the regulation and preservation of property (II, 3, 124) this role was one of trust construed through rational relations and ones' duties to God (II, 34).

5 See Maurice Ash *The Fabric of the World*, Resurgence Books, 1992, p.84.

6 From the Universal Declaration of Human Rights, General Assembly of the United Nations (UN) 10 December 1948.

7 Norberto Bobbio *The Age of Rights*, Polity Press, 1996, pp.44, 49

8 Hannah Arendt *The Human Condition*, University of Chicago Press, 1958, pp.164–165.

9 Milan Kundera *Immortality*, Faber, 1991, p.153.

10 Interests conceptualize problems, goals and means encountered by people in their use of rights and so is favoured here to the Hohfeldian conception of choice as the grounding characteristic or capacity for rights.

11 This is a slight caricature of Kant who, whilst having problems in grounding the motivation to the moral will in nothing more than a faith in
reason and at times being committed to a dualistic perspective which
cites reason outside of time and history, recognizes that our being moral
persons with the capacity for reasonableness and rationality involves
moments of sufficient determination, arenas of success where our willing
brings about specific achievements within phenomenal space. He distinguishes between public and private uses of reason; believing self-initiated
release from nonage to be unlikely the idea is to focus on public expressions of reason as critique rather than private uses of reason as instrumental. By conflating the two human rights discourse tends to promote
acquisitiveness as much as decency (*What is Enlightenment?* in H. Reiss
(ed.) *Kant's Political Writings*, Cambridge, 1991, p.57).

12 Stanley Benn 'Egalitarianism and the Equal Consideration of Interests' in
Nomos IX, New York University Press, pp.61–78, p.63.

13 Stanley Benn *A Theory of Freedom*, Cambridge University Press, 1988,
Ch.6.

14 Michael Freedon *Rights*, Open University Press, 1991, p.7.

15 Richard Flathman *The Practice of Rights*, Cambridge University Press,
1976, p.187.

16 Gilles Deleuze and Felix Guattari *What is Philosophy?* trans. Graham
Burchell and Hugh Tomlinson, Verso, 1994, p.31.

17 Immanuel Kant 'The Contest of the Faculties' in H. Reiss (ed.) *op. cit.*,
p.183.

18 See Norberto Bobbio *op. cit.*, pp.40–43, p.89.

19 In the conditions of modern society human rights are a particularly
appropriate mechanism to protect human dignity', Jack Donnelley, *op.
cit.*, p.122.

20 Three elements of autonomy outlined by Susan Mendus 'Colston Lecture'
in D. Milligan and W. Watts-Miller (eds) *Liberalism, Citizenship and
Autonomy*, Avebury, 1992, p.11.

21 Charles Taylor *Sources of the Self*, Cambridge University Press, 1989,
p.12.

22 United Nations Resolution 217, 10 December 1948.

23 Austin's concern for the human voice in ordinary language hastens after a
realization that in describing, proposing, questioning, arguing, listening
and the like we are not revealing truths or inhabiting tidy dictionaries
but inhabiting meanings. To attend to how we so speak is to be constantly aware of the fragility of language; of how easily we are bewitched.
This vulnerability is how language is fragmentary (see Stanley Cavell
'What did Derrida Want of Austin?' in his *Philosophical Passages.
Wittgenstein, Emerson, Austin, Derrida*, Blackwell, 1995, pp.55–61).

24 These comments are taken from Foucault's remarks on the modes
(criteria) used by social structures to develop monotonic rhythms to life
– stable unities in knowledge *created* by disciplinary power – see *Discipline and Punish*, Peregrine Books, 1985, pp.27–30.

25 Michel de Certeau *The Practice of Everyday Life*, University of California
Press, 1988, p.xiii.

26 Ibid., p.4.

27 C&V, p.63.

28 See G.H. Von Wright 'Wittgenstein in Relation to his Times' in B. McGuinness (ed.) *Wittgenstein and his Times*, Blackwell, 1982, pp.110–111.

29 Ibid., p.493.

30 Fania Pascal 'A Personal Memoir' in Rush Rhees (ed.) *Recollections of Wittgenstein*, Oxford, 1984, pp.34–36.

31 C&V, p.18e.

32 Foucault sees confession as a final act of acknowledgement of rightful authority by the condemned; the defining climax to the assertion of truth realized through the demonstrable infliction of pain and underlined by cleansing death (see *op. cit.*, Part 1).

33 Michel Foucault 'About the Beginning of the Hermeneutics of the Self' in *Political Theory*, Vol.21, No.2, May 1993, p.204.

34 Deleuze, Guattari and de Certeau talk of these trajectories which whilst reliant upon fields of capture for tethering go well beyond them into 'non-striated' space (see *op. cit.*).

35 See Paul Engelmann *Letters from Ludwig Wittgenstein*, Blackwell, 1967, p.78.

36 Ray Monk *Ludwig Wittgenstein: The Duty of Genius*, Vintage, 1991, pp.412–413.

37 C&V, p.27e

38 An attitude reminiscent of Thoreau's constant battle between his desire to end the hypocrisy of state control and his urge to desist from all involvement in public life: 'I came into this world, not chiefly to make this a good place to live in, but to live in it, be it good or bad' (H.D. Thoreau 'Civil Disobedience' in H Bedau (ed.) *Civil Disobedience*, Routledge, 1991, p.36).

39 Z, §440.

40 C&V, p.26e.

41 C&V, p.28e.

42 Errico Malatesta in G. Woodcock (ed.) *The Anarchist Reader*, Fontana, 1986, p.63.

43 Z, §374.

44 Z, §326.

45 Lyotard refers to this as *svelteness*, or wakefulness to the need for reciprocal adaptiveness in *Political Writings*, trans. Bill Readings and Kevin Paul Geiman, UCL Press, 1993, pp.25–29.

46 William Connolly talks of this in respect to the narcissistic traits of categorical imperatives. Citing Foucault and Nietzsche he effectively undermines the claims of such transcendentalists to universal relevance as merely veils behind which they hide their arrogance, 'Beyond Good and Evil' in *Political Theory*, Vol.2, No.3, August 1993, pp.365–389.

47 See Jean-François Lyotard 'Wittgenstein: After' in *Political Writings*, trans. B. Readings and K. Geiman, UCL Press, 1993, pp.20–24.

48 Adolf Loos invoked the same argument in architecture – the use of adornment in buildings characterized by the Secession movement leads to the confusion between art and culture; it smears naked reality with mystifying façades through a conflation of languages. It is more genuine to display new languages as they are with their new forms, methods, materials, techniques. The emphasis upon the use looks not upon adorn-

ment and tracery but function, no matter how stark (see Benedetto Gravagnuolo *Adolf Loos: Theory and Works*, trans. C.H. Evans, Locker Verlag, 1982, p.55).
49 PI, §620.

1 PRIVATE LANGUAGE . . .

1 T, 2.021.
2 T, 2.0271.
3 Paul Engelmann *Letters from Ludwig Wittgenstein*, Blackwell, 1967, p.101.
4 T, 1–2.0121.
5 NB, p.53e.
6 T, 6.124.
7 'Logic is not a body of doctrine, but a mirror image of the world', T, 6.13.
8 See Barry Allen *Truth in Philosophy*, Harvard University Press, 1995, pp.118–120.
9 T, 2.1, 2.11.
10 T, 2.151.
11 T, 2.172–2.174.
12 T, 2.202.
13 T, 2.1511.
14 T, 2.131.
15 Ibid., p.190. Also NB, appendix II, p.107:

> Logical so-called propositions *shew* [the] logical properties of language and therefore of [the] Universe, but *say* nothing . . . It is impossible to *say* what these properties are, because in order to do so, you would need a language, which hadn't got the properties in question, and it is impossible that this should be a *proper* language . . . In order that you should have a language which can express or *say* everything that *can* be said, this language must have certain properties; and when this is the case, *that* it has them can no longer be said in that language or *any* language.

16 T, 4.021.
17 This description is taken largely from Stephen Toulmin and Alan Janik *Wittgenstein's Vienna*, Weidenfeld and Nicholson, 1972, p.186.
18 T, 6.341–6.342.
19 T, 6.37.
20 T, 6.421.
21 NB, p.83e.
22 NB, p.85e. Wittgenstein reiterates this solipsistic view on p.82e ('The "I" of solipsism shrinks to an extensionless point and what remains is the reality co-ordinate with it').
23 T, 5.631.
24 T, 6.4321.
25 T, 6.422.
26 NB, p.79e.
27 T, 6.522.

28 Stephen Toulmin and Alan Janik, *op. cit.*, pp.192–196.
29 T, 6.41. The idea of value lying outside the world is what encouraged Wittgenstein's solipsism. My language being only that language I understand, that upon which I confer value, supposes that the limits of my language are the limits of my world. So far as acts are good and bad, then, they must change the world in that they change my perspective. Ethics is not about relations with others but the integrity of the self.
30 T, 6.43.
31 The links with Kant's practical reasoning here are striking. The phenomenal will (control of the body) never yields real knowledge for we can never *know*, we can never will something to be connected to our will as if it stands in relation to the world as does a stone, a limb or a telephone. The exercise of will as an ethical subject is less an action than a spiritual affirmation of self in self. It is no surprise that similar problematics encountered by Kant's separation of will and action ensue for the Tractatan view of language. Will requires an agreement with the world.
32 Søren Kierkegaard *The Journals*, trans. and ed. by Alexander Dru, Collins, 1958, p.43.
33 T, 6.4312.
34 See Yehuda Safran 'Adolf Loos: The Archimedian Point' in *The Architecture of Adolf Loos'*, Arts Council Catalogue, 1985, pp.26–35.
35 NB, p.81e.
36 Arthur Koestler 'Wittgensteinomania' in *The Heel of Achilles: Essays 1968–1973*, Hutchinson and Co., 1974, p.110.
37 Peter Winch 'Wittgenstein's Treatment of Will', in his *Ethics and Action*, Routledge, 1972, p.123.
38 Paul Engelmann suggests a similar influence/example was found in teaching schoolchildren, which gave Wittgenstein the practical experience of having to translate his thoughts into and receiving reaction from a language used by children. See *op. cit.*, p.115.
39 See Benedetto Gravagnuolo, *Adolf Loos: Theory and Work*, trans. C.H. Evans, Locker Verlag, 1982, p.19.
40 Ian Mortimer 'The Cathedral Builders', *Nexus*, No.4, November 1987, p.9.
41 'Only a very small part of architecture belongs to art: the tomb and the monument. Everything else, everything that serves a purpose, should be excluded from the realms of art', Loos quoted in K. Frampton *Modern Architecture*, Thames and Hudson, 3rd edn, 1992, p.92.
42 See Adolf 'Loos Architecture' in *The Architecture of Adolf Loos, op. cit.*, p.108.
43 Ibid., p.135.
44 Loos quoted in Benedetto Gravagnuolo, *op. cit.*, p. 46.
45 Bernard Williams 'Wittgenstein and Idealism' in *Royal Institute of Philosophy Lectures*, Vol.7, St Martin's Press, 1974, pp.75–80.
46 Taken from F.R. Leavis 'Memories of Wittgenstein' in R. Rhees (ed.) *Recollections of Wittgenstein*, Oxford, 1984, p.65.
47 Bernard Williams, *op. cit.*, p.82.
48 Discussed in Richard Flathman *Wilful Liberalism*, Cornell University Press, 1992, pp.54–55.
49 PI, §59.

50 PI, §16.
51 Francis Bacon identifies such problems in his figure 'the idol of the market place': he acutely observed that people had a tendency to think names inevitably refer to things when they do not or refer to things which necessarily remain ill-defined and confused. (Francis Bacon 'Of Nature in Men' in *Essays*, J. Parker and Son, 1860, p.419).
52 PI, §26.
53 PI, §§65–67.
54 PI, §67
55 PI, §77.
56 This is similar to Wittgenstein's statement in PI, II, xi, when asking of a picture of a triangle whether it is seen as hanging up, standing or falling over:

> Could I say what a picture must be like to produce this effect? No. There are, for example, styles of painting which do not convey anything to me in this immediate way, but do to other people. I think custom and upbringing have a hand in this.

To see things, aspects, we have to be immersed in practices of interaction, trial and error and education.
57 Gilles Deleuze and Felix Guattari *What is Philosophy?* trans. Graham Burchell and Hugh Tomlinson, Verso, 1994, p.24.
58 PI, §283.
59 PI, §182.
60 PI, §284.
61 PI, §§292–295.
62 BB, p.3.
63 Jeff Coulter *Mind in Action*, Polity Press, 1989, p.83.
64 Ibid., pp.84–86.
65 Z, §220.
66 Z, §304, §317.
67 PI, II, pp.222–225.
68 Z, §488, §491.
69 C&V, p.11e.
70 Z, §202.
71 OC, §504.
72 See Z, §§540–541, §545.
73 Z, §567, §577, §587.
74 Z, §§163–165.
75 See, for example, Bernard Williams, 'Left-Wing Wittgenstein, Right-Wing Marx', in *Common Knowledge*, Vol.1, No.1, Spring 1992, pp.33–42. What is natural is what we find to be so, and nothing more. Rather than trying to justify this feeling we must just try to get on living within it. All changes, thus, have to be based upon that understanding realizable only within a shared, social practice. As a consequence, all moral concepts remain rooted to specific linguistic contexts. Our ethical ideals are rooted in our ethical practices, and none can escape to obtain a universal relevance.
76 This being Bentham's position, rights are institutional creations conferred upon individuals informed by the teleological nature of human beings to

realize the good; tools of maximization and control rather than innate gifts.

77 Herbert Spencer *The Man Versus the State*, (1884) Penguin, 1969, p.167. Spencer uses sociological analysis of various 'ungoverned' tribes who despite their lack of institutional direction display rights-type behaviour in the ascription of property, truth and punishment. Societies embody private claims as a natural right, but one emerging from 'the natural relation between efforts and benefits' (p.179), not the timeless, natural character of the individual. Spencer emphasizes character in context.

78 Z, §556.

79 Wittgenstein's language games are reliant not upon inter-subjective agreement but agreement in forms of life, agreement in action, something which is altogether less deliberate. The social extends beyond the inter-subjective into the primitive, the traditional and the narrative.

80 Roger Trigg identifies this dispute as separate from that existing between materialists (who identify reality solely with what is observable) and idealists (those who see reality as composed purely through mental activity; the mind is all that exists). The realists' position is that there exists something which is real and independent from human knowledge. The anti-realists hold that nature is humanized through the representations manifest in people's attempts to seek a unity in the chaos through the imposition of organizational power. Trigg sees Wittgenstein as representative of the latter, as one who equates reality with 'reality-for-us', there being no being separate from 'being-as-expressed-in-ordinary-language'. See R. Trigg *Reality at Risk*, Harvester Wheatsheaf, 2nd edn, 1989, Ch.2 pp.30–39.

81 C&V, p.22e.

2 ... PUBLIC RULES

1 '[G]ood and evil only enter through the subject', NB, p.79.

2 PI, §269.

3 PI, §318.

4 G.P. Baker and P.M.S. Hacker *Scepticism, Rules and Language*, Blackwell, 1984, p.21.

5 S. Shanker *Wittgenstein and the Turning Point in the Philosophy of Mathematics*, Croom Helm, 1987, p.56.

6 RFM, VI, §48.

7 RFM, VI, §47.

8 See G. Baker and P. Hacker, *op. cit.*, p.43.

9 PI, §198.

10 RFM, V, §45.

11 WL, p.155.

12 RFM, V, §45.

13 S. Shanker, *op. cit.*, p.67.

14 PI, §198.

15 RFM, V, §46.

16 RFM, VI, §59.

17 PI, §322.

18 Z, §567.
19 See also Peter Winch *Trying to Make Sense*, Blackwell, Oxford, 1987, p.7.
20 'In so far as I do intend the construction of a sentence in advance, that is made possible by the fact that I can speak the language in question "such that" . . . in order to *want* to say something one must also have mastered a language', PI, §§337–338.
21 Michel Foucault – as discussed in B. Willis, introduction. to *Art after Modernism* (1984), New Museum of Contemporary Art, NY, 1989, pp.x–xviii.
22 Michel Foucault *The Order of Things*, Tavistock, 1977, p.161.
23 Keith Thomas *Man and the Natural World*, Penguin, 1984.
24 Michel Foucault, *op. cit.*, p.162.
25 Ibid., p.163.
26 RFM, I, §32.
27 PI, §65.
28 PI, II, xi, p.224e.
29 Z, §440.
30 PI, §85.
31 PI, §198.
32 PI, §197.
33 See in Sabina Lovibond *Realism and Imagination and Ethics*, Blackwell, 1983, footnote p.189.
34 PI, §242.
35 PI, §241.
36 RFM, VI, §42.
37 Games can be learnt without ever having learnt or formulated rules but by watching how the aspects of the game fit together; however this is only possible if the watcher already knows what a game is in the first place, that he has previously understood similar things, PI, §31.
38 RFM, III, §§35–36.
39 RFM, I, §§4–6.
40 See, for example, Norman Malcolm 'Wittgenstein on Language and Rules' in *Philosophy*, No.64, January 1989, pp.5–28 and R. Fogelin *Wittgenstein*, (1976) RKP, 1987.
41 G. Baker and P. Hacker, *op. cit.*, and in 'Malcolm on Language and Rules' in *Philosophy*, No.65, April 1990, pp.167–179.
42 See T.S. Champlin in 'Solitary Rule Following' in *Philosophy*, Vol.67, No.261, July 1992. He distinguishes between a non-normative and normative rule, saying that the latter is that which persists in a custom, the former being found in habits (p.293). Customs rely upon an agreement found amongst us (p.298).
43 G. Baker and P. Hacker *Skepticism, Rules and Language*, *op. cit.*, pp.85–90.
44 Ibid., pp. 61–77.
45 G. Baker and P. Hacker 'Malcolm on Language and Rules', *op. cit.*, p.170.
46 RFM, VII, §60.
47 Z, §428.
48 Z, §431.

49 Z, §436.
50 See Cora Diamond 'Rules, Looking in the Right Places' in D.Z. Phillips and P. Winch (eds) *Wittgenstein: Attention to Particulars*, Macmillan, 1989, p.19.
51 We say things like this is so and so, and we have no right to say them as such, but we still do 'For of course I don't make use of the agreement of human beings to affirm identity. What criterion do you use then? None at all. To use the word without a justification does not mean to use it wrongly' (RFM, V, §33).
52 S. Shanker (*op. cit.*, p.21) supports this conclusion with manuscript evidence of Wittgenstein's which points to his conceiving a Crusoe character as being able to play language games with himself. To envisage someone following a rule we do not have to be able to impose our normative standards upon her behaviour but only recognize a complexity in her behaviour that is indicative of normative regularity.
53 G. Baker and P. Hacker *Scepticism, Rules and Language*, *op. cit.*, p.171.
54 Ibid., p.178.
55 OC, §509–510.
56 PI, II, xi.
57 See S. Lovibond, *op. cit.*, p.150.
58 For a good discussion of this see Newton Garver 'Naturalism and Transcendendality: The Case of "Form of Life"' in S.Tougherin (ed.) *Wittgenstein and Contemporary Philosophy*, Thoemmes Press, 1994 pp.58–63.
59 See S. Shanker, *op. cit.*, pp.320–321.
60 OC, §530.
61 OC, §359.
62 OC, §105. See also R. Monk *Ludwig Wittgenstein: The Duty of Genius*, Vintage, 1991, p.563.
63 RFM, I, 34.
64 S. Shanker, *op. cit.*, p.56.
65 OC, §509. Something equally well articulated in PI, II, xi: 'My attitude towards him is an attitude towards a soul. I am not of the *opinion* that he has a soul.'
66 C&V, p.45e.
67 T, 6.51.
68 Z, §410.
69 OC, §§94–95.
70 Z, §289.
71 Proper names have reference fixed through family resemblance and elastic rules – there is never any one specific description because reference is fixed by relations between the speaker of the name and their environment. Such relations are best understood not by reference to mental states of the speaker but by their acquisition and use of the name. Thus, as well as inference, belief and discrimination influencing reference, the natural and social environment also plays an important role (see Tylor Burge 'Philosophy of Language and Mind' in *The Philosophical Review*, Vol.101, No.1, January 1992, pp.3–51 (pp.23–25).
72 OC, §315.
73 R. Flathman *Wilful Liberalism*, Cornell University Press, 1992, p.60.

74 OC, §§616, 617.
75 RC, p.4e.
76 See H. Turnbull *The Great Mathematicians*, Methuen, 1962, p.50.
77 PI, II, xii.
78 OC, §§95, 271.
79 RFM, VI, §26.
80 RFM, VI, §40.
81 RFM, VI, §46.
82 PI, II, xi, p.225e.
83 C, §§96–98.
84 RFM, I, §121.
85 OC, §344.
86 RFM, I, §63, §74.
87 PI, §415. See also RFM, I, §141.
88 OC, §105.
89 RFM, I, §152.
90 OC, §370.
91 OC, §475.
92 Z, §391.
93 C&V, p.31e.
94 LA, p.3.
95 G. Baker and P. Hacker *Wittgenstein: Rules, Grammar and Necessity*, Blackwell, 1985, p.240.
96 Wittgenstein tries not to justify this by reference to nature: 'But our interest does not fall back upon these possible causes of the function of concepts; we are not doing natural science, nor yet natural history – since we can also invent fictitious natural history for our own purposes' (PI, II, xii).
97 Z, §326.
98 LA, p.2.
99 See Stanley Cavell on this reading of the *Philosophical Investigations* where he talks of the builders as being somehow unfree – theirs is a world in which we are not sure whether we know our way about, *Philosophical Passages*, Blackwell, 1995, pp.156–166.
100 PI, §206, §207.
101 RFM, VII, §§59–60.
102 The *Brown Book*, along with *Remarks on Frazer's Golden Bough*, are replete with exhortations to the reader to 'Imagine that . . .'; 'Imagine a people . . .'; 'Imagine a language . . .'; 'Imagine that humans were . . .'; 'Imagine this case . . .'; 'Imagine a tribe . . .' (see, for example, BB, §§44–66) in order that they may comprehend correspondences *and* distinctions in ways of being.
103 Thus though Wittgenstein's explorer occupies a similar position to Donald Davidson's radical translator in that they both assume that it is part of the natural expression of individuals to act regularly (that what they intend ('p') is how they act (*p*) and that state of affairs (p) is brought about), the two differ in their view of what constitutes this regularity. Wittgenstein sees the explorer as being able to assume that the tribe's intentions to act correspond with their actions because the observable regularity in action reveals an agreement in form of life, whereas for

Davidson it is agreement in rationality. Davidson sees radically different conceptual systems precluded by the principle of charity: we have to assume that in the majority of cases people have a logically and rationally coherent set of beliefs which, for the most part, are true. This is not to say that they are never wrong, but that the context of ascribing a mistake will only allow us to go so far in recognizing error before we begin seriously to question the correctness of our own interpretations of their beliefs. Thus there can be no mind radically different from our own because minds are what we attribute to people when we interpret their action in rational terms. There are no minds outside of minds-as-we-rationally-understand-them because, as Michael Root says of Davidson's schema, we understand as agent a self who is able to understand and conform to the interpretative norms of rationality (see M. Root 'Davidson and Social Science' in E. LePore (ed.) *Truth and Interpretation*, Blackwell, 1986, p.295). We can understand other languages to a greater or lesser degree but no language is impossible to translate. Now Wittgenstein would agree that because all languages have the normative requirement of displaying regularity then all are recognizable as languages, but his explorer is placed in the far less certain position of recognizing only the potential normative regularity from the perspective of their own training, and not the commensurability of concepts used. For Wittgenstein translation depends upon awareness of the role the word plays in the whole life of the tribe. It is in this sense that if a lion could speak we would not understand it.

104 Z, §388.
105 Z, §374.
106 Maurice Ash *Journey into the Eye of the Needle*, Green Books, 1989, p.37.
107 PI, §102.
108 C&V, p.44e.

3 LINGUISTIC SELVES

1 See Gilles Deleuze and Felix Guattari *What is Philosophy?*, Verso, 1994, p.8.
2 PI, II, pp.199e–200e.
3 PI, II, p.208e.
4 LA, I, §15.
5 See Michel de Certeau *Heterologies: Discourse on the Other*, Manchester University Press, 1986, pp.42–44.
6 Stanley Cavell *Philosophical Passages*, Blackwell, 1995, pp.168–170.
7 See Stephen Mulhall 'Remonstrations: Heidegger, Derrida and Wittgenstein's Hand' in *Journal of the British Society for Phenomenology*, Vol.26, No.1, January 1995, pp.65–85.
8 PI, §90, §97.
9 Michel de Certeau *The Practice of Everyday Life*, University of California Press, 1988, pp.34–39.
10 Ibid., pp.29–30.

11 See M. Hodges 'The Status of Ethical Judgements' in *Philosophical Investigations*, Vol.18, No.2, April 1995, pp.99–122.

12 Derrida casts this as the undecidability of structure and non-totalizability of language where the vocative and accusative collide – language is unable to totalize itself (see R. Smith *Derrida and Autobiography*, Cambridge University Press, 1995, pp.119–121).

13 PI, II, p.207e.

14 PI, II, p.213e.

15 *De Stijl* occupies a seminal place in the historical exposition of aesthetic expressions and their relations to the form, articulating as it does the idea that it is only through the work of art itself, through learning, contemplation, comparison and use that the new can be *seen*. The final abandonment of the curve for the straight line, the reduction of the spectrum to primary colour and form to geometric shape attempt to show immutable plastic relations, the ultimate harmony and constant equilibrium of pure relations between man and nature. That this results in an entirely abstract totality, arising from the tragedy of life, suggests it remains something both beholden to, and never entirely free from, form (see Theo van Doesberg *Principles of Neo-Plastic Art*, Lund Humphries, 1969).

16 Nietzsche's conception of will evokes this complexity of sensation, recognition and emotion articulated through action whereby we both command something within ourselves *and* obey through a knowledge of the constraints and pressures by which that command is articulated. That we deceive ourselves as to this complexity with the synthetic term 'I' creates the illusion that willing *alone* suffices for action (*Beyond Good and Evil*, George Allen and Unwin, 1967, pp.25–28).

17 This discussion of *Beyond Good and Evil* (especially §19) owes much to David Owen *Nietzsche, Politics and Modernity*, Sage, 1996, pp.56–67.

18 PI, II, p.228e.

19 Stephen Mulhall, *op. cit.*, pp.60–64.

20 RFM, VI, §47.

21 RFM, VI, §60.

22 Although primarily concerned with addressing mathematical problems outlined by Hilbert, Turing's work is relevant in that by developing a machine capable of reading and processing information (one which he later built, the first computer) he addressed the possibility of defining human calculation in mechanical terms, of equating the logical pattern of the mind to that of abstract, soon to become real, machines. An accessible discussion can be found in Andrew Hodge's biography of Turing, *The Enigma of Intelligence*, Unwin, 1986, pp.90–110.

23 Alan Turing 'Computers, Machinery and Intelligence' in *Mind*, Vol.LXI, No.236, 1950.

24 Although Turing's machine was hypothetical, today there are computers set up with 'neural simulations' which spot patterns in images and events and so can learn how people react in order that they may continue in a similar fashion without external inputs.

25 Stuart Shanker 'Wittgenstein versus Turing on the Nature of Church's Thesis' in *Notre Dame Journal of Formal Logic*, Vol.28, No.4, October 1987.

26 Turing quoted in ibid., p.633.

27 Thought is a process of dignification to which only humans have access (Stuart Shanker *Wittgenstein and the Turning Point in the Philosophy of Mathematics*, Croom Helm, 1987, pp.20–22). To say this is not to decry the ability of machines to perform in valuable or destructive ways; they are powerful, and to say that they cannot think is to impose no limitation upon them whatsoever, just as it is no limitation upon a natural scientist that he cannot be God.

28 See, for example, work by Timothy Lenoir, which shows how recent work in science is orientated less around paradigm clashing or falsification procedure than the linking of theory and experiment through selective models based not on sense data but publicly defeasible, noteworthy, stable events containable within existing available experimental apparatus. Phenomena are not discovered, but created by localized laboratories immersed in tradition and repertoire. It is intellectually deficient to see science as expressing a logically closed relation between theory and experiment – phenomena, as much as human selves, are context specific, they are tied in with criterial ascription, rules of representation and forms (Timothy Lenoir 'Practice, Reason, Context: The Dialogue between Theory and Experiment' in *Science in Context*, Vol.1, No.2, 1988, pp. 3–22).

29   'I am leaving the room because you tell me to.'/'I am leaving the room but not because you tell me to.'/Does this proposition *describe* a connexion between my action and his order; or does it make the connexion?

Can one ask: 'How do you know that you do it because of this, or not because of this?' And the answer perhaps 'I feel it'?

(PI, §487)

30 The trouble with the question 'Is it possible for a machine to think?'

is not really that we don't yet know a machine which could do the job. The question is not analogous to that which someone might have asked a hundred years ago: 'Can a machine liquefy a gas?' The trouble is rather that the sentence, 'A machine thinks (perceives, wishes)' seems somehow nonsensical. It is as though we had asked 'Has the number 3 a colour?' (What colour could it be, as it obviously has none of the colours known to us?)

(BB, p.48)

31 Cornelius Castoriadis 'Radical Imagination and the Social Instituting Imaginary' in G. Robinson and J. Randel (eds) *Rethinking Imagination: Culture and Creativity*, Routledge, 1994, p.144.

32 Michel de Certeau *The Practice of Everyday Life, op. cit.*, p.33.

33 PI, §107.

34 See Anthony Kenny 'Wittgenstein and the Nature of Philosophy' in Brian MacGuinness (ed.) *Wittgenstein and his Times*, Blackwell, 1982, p.19.

35 C&V, p.37e.

36 C&V, p.5e.

37 BB, pp.48–50.

38 Rush Rhees 'Wittgenstein on Language and Ritual' in Brian MacGuiness (ed.), *op. cit.*, p.93.

39 Sigmund Freud *Totem and Taboo*, Pelican, 1937, p.170.

40 Ibid., pp.200–202.
41 It seems no coincidence that Freud ends his text with the quote from Goethe which Wittgenstein found so arresting: 'In the beginning was the deed', ibid., p.246.
42 LA, p.42.
43 LA, p.51.
44 Herbert Marcuse is typical of this paradoxically blinkered reading of Wittgenstein. See his *One Dimensional Man*, Ark, 1986, pp.170–185.
45 Ernest Gellner *Reason and Culture*, Blackwell, 1992, p.121.
46 Stanley Cavell *Conditions Handsome and Unhandsome: The Carus Lectures 1988*, University of Chicago Press, 1990, p.97.
47 C&V p.64e.
48 C&V p.35e.
49 Jane Heal *Fact and Meaning*, Blackwell, 1989, p.149.
50 Richard Rorty 'Is Natural Science a Natural Kind?' in *Objectivity, Relativism and Truth*, Cambridge, 1991, p.60.
51 See R. Alva Noë 'Wittgenstein, Phenomenology and What it Makes Sense to Say' in *Philosophy and Phenomenological Research*, Vol.LIV, No.1, March 1994, pp.1–42, p.27.
52 A detailed and sensitively argued account of the persistent core is found in Vinit Haksar *Indivisible Selves and Moral Practice*, Barnes and Noble, 1991, pp.53–55.
53 Robert Nozick *Anarchy, State and Utopia*, Blackwell, 1988, p.168.
54 Pascal *Pensées*, trans. J. Warrington, Everyman, 1973, §167.
55 Ibid., §141.
56 BB, pp.64–66.
57 PI, II, iv.
58 BB, p.62.
59 C&V, p.53e.
60 Stanley Cavell 'Availability of Wittgenstein's Later Philosophy' in G. Pitcher (ed.) *Wittgenstein: The Philosophical Investigations*, University of Notre Dame Press, 1966, pp.170–172.

4 LIBERAL AND PRAGMATIC FORMS

1 Michael Oakeshott sees all moral rules as deliberatively and not demonstratively influential; abstractions deriving their force from the practice as spoken language and not as *sui generis* commands. See *On Human Conduct*, Oxford University Press, 1975, pp.67–68.
2 Seamus Heaney *The Redress of Poetry*, Faber, 1995, p.xvii.
3 See Paul Johnson *The Inner and Outer*, Routledge, 1994, pp.108–111.
4 Bernard Williams 'Persons, Character and Morality' in *Moral Luck*, Cambridge University Press, 1981, pp.1–19.
5 PI, §203.
6 The concept of negative rights implies that nothing more is required of others in relation to the rights claimant than forbearance, the duty not to interfere, whereas this language game of respect very often requires the use of many resources: police, systems of law, diplomatic treaties,

institutional buildings and so on (see Henry Shue *Basic Rights*, Princeton University Press, 1980, pp.35–64).

7 Ronald Dworkin sees such equality of respect and concern as the fundamental tenet of liberal thinking – only through such equality can we recognize liberty (see 'Liberalism' in his *A Matter of Principle*, Cambridge University Press, 1985, pp.188–192).

8 John Rawls *A Theory of Justice*, Harvard University Press, 1971, pp.10–13.

9　　For if the law is such that a whole people could not *possibly* agree to it (for example, if it stated that a certain class of *subjects* must be privileged as a hereditary *ruling class*) it is unjust; but if it is at least *possible* that a people could agree to it, it is our duty to consider the law as just, even if the people were in such a position or attitude of mind that they would probably refuse their consent if they were consulted.

　　(Kant quoted in Jeremy Waldron *Liberal Rights*, Cambridge University Press, 1993, p.52)

Our individuality and reason is given prior to social relationships of power and subordination and so ethical law is independent of existing conceptions of the good; it is based on reason alone, and this secures the primacy of human rights. The individual as rational, as moral, is seen somehow as separate from the individual as experiencing everyday life (see V. Seidler *Kant, Respect and Injustice*, RKP, 1990, Ch.8).

10 Stanley Benn *A Theory of Freedom*, Cambridge University Press, 1988, pp.92–98.

11 Tom Regan *The Case for Animal Rights*, Routledge, 1988, p.236.

12 Joel Feinberg *Social Philosophy*, Prentice Hall, 1973, Ch.6, where he talks of worth being a non-meritous, non-grading concept attributable to those able to perceive of themselves at a meta-level and so be able to follow the rational precepts of the Golden Rule.

13 Ronald Dworkin, *op. cit.*, p.48. People should be able to give content to their own lives by making their own commitments to act, to take on responsibility based upon critical self-reflection and to be morally autonomous, something which involves people, in the Kantian sense of using their practical rationality, in determining for themselves the nature of moral reasons and principles upon which they should act.

14 BB, pp.15–19.

15 PI, II, ix.

16 Heidegger, quoted in Robert Pippin *Modernism as a Philosophical Problem*, Blackwell, 1991, p.122.

17 Amy Baker *The Psychological Underpinnings of Nietzsche's Doctrine of the 'Will to Power'*, MSc Philosophy Thesis, LSE, September 1992, p.6.

18 Nietzsche calls the capacity the 'plastic power' to incorporate in themselves what is past and foreign, the ability to heal wounds, to adapt and, above all, to draw clearly marked horizons, limits to the self (Nietzsche 'On the Uses and Disadvantages of History for Life', in *Untimely Meditations*, trans. R.J. Hollingdale, Cambridge University Press, 1983, pp.62–63). The plastic art is being sensitive to when it is appropriate to act historically and when it is appropriate to act unhistorically. To act out

of intense consciousness, according to some intense, divine meaning from within needs to be seen in conjunction with the act of historical awareness, our appreciation of the linguistic and partial struggle of living with a narrative past. The living self with its inner drive to construct and the historical narrative must live in equilibrium.

19 Amy Baker, *op. cit.*, p.34.
20 Cornelius Castoriadis 'The Social Historical' in *Philosophy, Politics and Autonomy*, Oxford University Press, 1991, p.38.
21 Ibid., p.39.
22 Jeremy Waldron, *op. cit.*, p.345.
23 See John Rawls 'The Basic Liberties and Their Priority' in S.M. McMurrin (ed.) *Liberty, Equality and the Law: Selected Tanner Lectures on Moral Philosophy*, Cambridge University Press, 1987.
24 Cornelius Castoriadis 'The Nature and Value of Equality' *op. cit.*, pp.141–142.
25 John Rawls *A Theory of Justice*, *op. cit.*, pp.302–303.
26 John Rawls 'The Basic liberties and Their Priority' *op. cit.*, p.22.
27 Ibid., p.14.
28 Ibid., p.21.
29 John Rawls *A Theory of Justice*, *op. cit.*, pp.447–477.
30 Rawls equates them to members of a family where no single element is superior but have to adjust to one another in order to guarantee their central range in the protection of the moral powers (ibid., p.72).
31 J.S. Mill 'Spirit of the Age' in G. Williams (ed.) *J.S. Mill on Politics and Society*, Fontana, 1976, pp.170–178.
32 John Rawls 'Justice as Fairness: Political not Metaphysical' in *Philosophy and Public Affairs*, Vol.14, No.3, 1985, pp.223–251; 'The Idea of an Overlapping Consensus' in *Oxford Journal of Legal Studies*, Vol.7, No.1, 1987, pp. 1–25; 'The Priority of Right and Ideas of the Good' in *Philosophy and Public Affairs*, Vol.17, No.4, 1988, pp. 251–276; and *Political Liberalism*, Columbia University Press, 1993.
33 See John Rawls in 'The Idea of an Overlapping Consensus', *op. cit.*, p.6.
34 Here the OP asks contractors not to choose principles but to choose those principles to which they would be committed under all circumstances – it is a conditioned, not a free choice, reflecting Rawls' highest-order interests in a specific form of life.
35 John Rawls 'Reply to Habermas' in *The Journal of Philosophy*, Vol.XCII, No.3, March 1995, pp.132–180, p.153.
36 Ibid., p.156.
37 Ibid., p.139.
38 Ibid., p.165.
39 There are goods which can only be enjoyed as part of group consciousness. Individuals, though they relate themselves to these goods in a specific way, experience it as an aspect of others' similar experience. The worth of the experience is inseparable from the group (Jeremy Waldron 'Communal Goods as Human Rights' *op. cit.*, pp.354–358).
40 The idea of consensus is not the melding or abridgement of specific, identifiable interests but agreement to which all interests would subscribe, irrespective of their being.

41 John Rawls 'Reply to Habermas', *op. cit.*, p.134.
42 John Rawls 'The Law of Peoples' in Stephen Shute and Susan Hurley (eds) *Human Rights: The Oxford Amnesty Lectures 1993*, Basic Books, 1993, p.43.
43 John Rawls 'Reply to Habermas' *op. cit.*, p.135.
44 Stephen Mulhall and Adam Swift *Liberals and Communitarians*, Blackwell, 1992, pp.188–190.
45 John Rawls 'The Law of Peoples', *op. cit.*, p.46.
46 John Rawls 'Reply to Habermas', *op. cit.*, p.173, p.179.
47 Stephen Mulhall and Adam Swift, *op. cit.*, p.187.
48 Jeremy Waldron, *op. cit.*, p.191.
49 Cornelius Castoriadis 'The Nature and Value of Equality', *op. cit.*, pp.121–123.
50 Murray Bookchin, in *The Ecology of Freedom*, Black Rose Books (revised edn) 1991, distinguishes between justice, which he sees as formal equality before the law and the ethics of intellectual reason, and substantive equality which recognizes the subjectivity and heterogeneity of peoples. Contract theorists like Rawls standardize everything to the level of rational egoism – we all display maximin rationality, we all have equal access to social knowledge, we are all in possession of the two moral powers and so on. Such homogeneity, argues Bookchin, ignores the very real distinctions between people. Real justice should recognize the differences, the variety and complexity within the *polis*. Bookchin is making an important point; when the rule of equivalence ceases to be an issue of compensation (because, rather than looking at the differences between people and compensating them it emphasizes their similarities) and becomes one of balance, inequalities can arise through the fetishization of needs by envisaging them in purely material terms (pp.142–147).
51 Following from Paine's formulation of government as being built upon the bowers of the ruins of paradise.
52 Stephen Mulhall *Promising, Consent and Citizenship: Rawls and Cavell on Morality and Politics*, unpublished manuscript, p.15.
53 Thinkers like Machiavelli and Mill also found the interplay of critical ideas, the antagonism between groups, the open-endedness of purposes and techniques as integral to the promotion of good living. *Virtu*, felt Machiavelli, could only be kept alive through the vigorous vigilance necessary in the face of opposition; only then are people not taken in by the whims, hostilities and capricious nature of *Fortuna*; it is through struggle that meaning is given to ethical creeds (see *Mill On Liberty*, Everyman, 1954, p.99); without the challenge of open discussion they are dead, habit-forming. In no longer having to defend the truth it loses its focus (p.104). There is almost an alchemical analysis going on here whereby through collision and chaos we get purity and clarity.
54 PI, §326.
55 Cornelius Castoriadis 'The Greek Polis and the Creation of Democracy', *op. cit.*, p.100.
56 Ibid., p.113.
57 See John Rawls in 'Justice as Fairness: Political not Metaphysical' *op. cit.*, p.249.

58 Cornelius Castoriadis in 'Individual, Society, Rationality, History', *op. cit.*, pp.62–65.

59 Michel Foucault 'The Subject and Power' in H. Dreyfus and T. Rabinow *Michel Foucault: Beyond Structurarlism and Hermenentics*, University of Chicago Press, 1983, p. 227.

60 Franz Kafka *The Great Wall of China*, Penguin, 1986, p.73.

61 Elizabeth Wolgast *The Grammar of Justice*, Cornell University Press, 1987, p.41.

62 C&V, p. 87e.

63 Ibid., p.193.

64 Richard Rorty in 'Introduction' to *Objectivity, Relativism and Truth*, Cambridge, 1991, p.10.

65 Richard Rorty *Contingency, Irony and Solidarity*, Cambridge University Press, 1989, p.93.

66 Richard Rorty, *Objectivity, Relativism and Truth*, *op. cit.*, p.12.

67 Ibid., p.199.

68 Ibid., p.27.

69 See David Hall *Richard Rorty*, SUNY Press, 1994, p.104, where the concept 'vagueness' is disolved into the semantic (the number of possible interpretations); the literal (conceptual openness as in love, infinity, etc.); the historic (presence of counter-narrative); metaphorical (disturbing); and pragmatic (the number of possible actions occasioned by the word). All of these Hall identifies as aspects of what Rorty conceives as the exploitation of text and lumps.

70 In Ray Monk's biography of Wittgenstein (*Ludwig Wittgenstein: The Duty of Genius*, Vintage, 1991, p.282) there is a reference to the sympathetic attitude Wittgenstein took towards 'spiritual' thinkers such as Heidegger who found themselves at the edge of language, points where we can go no further; they become engaged in a struggle with language in which they need to recognize 'The limit of language is shown by its being impossible to describe the fact which corresponds to (is the translation of) a sentence, without simply repeating the sentence' (C&V, p.10e).

71 Rorty sees irony as a compilation of gravity and frivolity which enables the few strong poets amongst us to continually bring into question processes of socialization and equilibrium through continual redescription at a private level. This redescription is possible because Rorty no longer takes a Tractatan view of language as being confined to a technical role, as something which cannot express value. Indeed, it is the very poetic qualities of language that precipitate such iconoclastic and novel language games. Language is not so much value free as value sodden with poetic metaphor, totally aesthetic as opposed to mechanical – and with this language of irony we realize that there is nothing out there that makes our grammatical positions right, just or rational. Claims to certainty are not stable, as Wittgenstein said; sometimes the 'facts' buck and we are left unseated, but like the thrill of riding the bronco, the ironist revels in this erratic and sometimes furious movement (see an expanded discussion of Rorty's views on irony in David Hall, *op. cit.*, pp.129–168).

72 Ibid., p.97.

73 Ibid., p.99.

74 Rorty is echoing Mill's fear here (citing de Tocqueville), that 'As democracy advances, the opinions of mankind on most subjects of general interest will become, he believes, as compared with any former period, more rooted and more difficult to change; and mankind more and more in danger of losing the moral courage and pride of independence which make them deviate from the beaten path either in speculation or in conduct', thereby allowing government more and more control in order 'to relieve mankind from the care of their own interests, and keep them under a type of tutelage' ('M. de. Tocqueville on Democracy in America' in G. Williams (ed.), *op. cit.*, p.231). Rather than rely on rights to allay this trend Rorty believes we have to look outside of political or ethical concepts altogether, and towards poetry and art. In a curious echo of Wittgenstein's early views he asks us to acknowledge that creative value lies, if anywhere, with those who inhabit private realms of the ineffable.

76 'Autonomy is not something which all human beings have within them and which society can release by ceasing to repress them. It is something which certain particular human beings hope to attain by self-creation, and which few actually do' (Richard Rorty *Contingency, Irony and Solidarity*, *op. cit.*, p.65).

76 See Wyndham Lewis *The Art of Being Ruled*, Chatto and Windus, 1926, p.127.

77 See David Hall, *op. cit.*, p.180.

78 Richard Rorty 'On Human Rights' in Stephen Shute and Susan Hurley (eds), *op. cit.*, p.124.

79 Richard Rorty, *Contingency, Irony and Solidarity*, *op. cit.*, p.80.

80 Ibid., p.94.

81 Ibid., pp.67–68.

82 Rorty's appreciation of grammatical embeddedness is not a communitarian commitment to the need for communal succour. Communitarians like MacIntyre find something intrinsically loathsome and isolationist in the liberal character which they see as making tacit overtures to essentialist metaphysics. Rorty, however, is prepared to accept the liberal self without appealing to *any* theory of human nature; believing the priority of democracy to philosophy to be sufficient for most people to get on with their lives free from intolerance and communal suffocation (see David Hall, *op. cit.*, pp.101–103).

83 Richard Rorty, *Objectivity, Relativism and Truth*, *op. cit.*, p.184.

84 Ibid., p.181.

5 IRONY AND THE ART OF LIVING

1 'What our future rulers will be like will not be determined by any large, necessary truths about human nature and its relation to truth and justice, but by a lot of small contingent facts' (Richard Rorty *Contingency, Irony and Solidarity*, Cambridge University Press, 1989, p.6).

2 Ibid., p.16.

3 Richard Rorty *Objectivity, Relativism and Truth*, Cambridge University Press, 1991 p.10.
4 Richard Rorty quoted in David Hall *Richard Rorty*, SUNY Press, 1994, p.202.
5 Richard Rorty *Objectivity, Relativism and Truth*, op. cit., p.192.
6 Ibid., p.194.
7 Ibid., p.190.
8 Richard Rorty *Contingency, Irony and Solidarity*, op. cit., p.75.
9 OC, §344.
10 Richard Rorty *Contingency, Irony and Solidarity*, op. cit., p.80.
11 For a clear summary of this aspect of Rorty's philosophy see Kai Nielsen 'An UnRortyan Defence of Rorty in *Inquiry*, Vol.39, No.1, March 1996, pp.71–96.
12 Rorty is following on from Wittgenstein's observations on objecthood here; 'We have a colour system as we have a number system. Do the systems reside in *our* nature or in the nature of things? How are we to put it? – *Not* in the nature of things' (Z, §357).
13 Richard Rorty 'Is Truth a Goal of Enquiry? Davidson vs Wright' in *Philosophical Quarterly*, Vol. 45, No.180, July 1995, pp.281–300.
14 Richard Rorty *Contingency, Irony and Solidarity*, op. cit., p.84.
15 Ibid., p.216.
16 Richard Rorty 'Cosmopolitanism without Emancipation' in *Objectivity, Relativism and Truth*, op. cit., p.215.
17 Richard Rorty *Contingency, Irony and Solidarity*, op. cit., p.86.
18 Ibid., p.209.
19 Rorty identifies Orwell's O'Brien as one such sadistic fantasy – one reminding us of how peculiarly with humans we are creatures who can be 'humiliated by the forcible tearing down of particular structures of language and belief in which they were socialized', ibid., p.177.
20 Judith Shklar *Ordinary Vices*, Harvard University Press, 1984, p.8.
21 Richard Rorty, *Contingency, Irony and Solidarity*, op. cit., p.198.
22 Richard Rorty 'On Human Rights' in Stephen Shute and Susan Hurley (eds) *Human Rights: The Oxford Amnesty Lectures 1993*, Basic Books, 1993, p.115.
23 Ibid., p.128.
24 It is interesting to note that ironic poets could conceivably have as much difficulty in 'getting real' as do, according to Aristotle, Plato's philosopher kings.
25 Rorty talks of Freud as a great reveller of the poetic but limits this widening of perspectivism to a psychological fantasy. It is the creative unconsciousness which is democratized, not the active language user – see 'The Contingency of Selfhood' in *Contingency, Irony and Solidarity*, op. cit., pp.23–43.
26 C&V, p.32e.
27 The grammatical context does not necessarily involve the Proustian engagement with the past:

> for ever squatting in the tepid bath of his remembered past. And all the stale soapsuds of countless previous washings floated around him, all the accumulated dirt of years lay crusty on the sides of the tub or

hung in dark suspension in the water. And there he sat, a pale repellent invalid, taking up spongefuls of his own thick soup and squeezing it over his face.

(Aldous Huxley *Eyeless in Gaza*, Chatto and Windus, 1936, p.9)

Traditions and memories are open components of individual self-assertion which resists the passive soaking in a cultural heritage but an embrace of the potential for instituting as well as the instituted.

28 See Cornelius Castoriadis 'The Sayable and the Unsayable' in *Cross-roads in the Labyrinth*, Harvester, 1984, p.138.

29 See Gilles Deleuze and Felix Guattari who in *A Thousand Plateaus* (trans. Brian Massumi, University of Minnesota Press, 1987, pp.2–5) talk of rhyzomic assemblages, open-ended multiplicities defined by absence and limits in contrast to those of an arboreal nature, hierarchical, foundational and rigidified.

30 Richard Rorty 'On Human Rights', *op. cit.*, p.122.

31 Richard Rorty *Objectivity, Relativism and Truth*, *op. cit.*, p.219.

32 For an extended discussion of this see David Owen *Nietzsche, Politics and Modernity*, Sage, 1996, p.120.

33 Wittgenstein quoted in R. Harris *Language, Saussure and Wittgenstein*, RKP, 1990, p.41.

34 See Stanley Cavell *Must We Mean What We Say?*, Charles Scribner, 1969, pp.49–50.

35 PI, II, i p.225e.

36 Cornelius Castoriadis in preface to *Cross-roads in the Labyrinth*, *op. cit.*, pp.xxiii–xxix.

37 A. Wellmer 'Intersubjectivity and Reason' in L. Hertzberg and J. Pietarinen (eds) *Perspectives on Human Conduct*, E.J. Brill, 1988, pp.154–155. The point is made by Wittgenstein: 'I once said, perhaps rightly: The earlier culture will become a heap of rubble and finally a heap of ashes, but spirits will hover over the ashes', C&V, p.3e.

38 By this I refer to democratic rather than consociational pluralism; although liberalism is tolerant it seeks to assimilate people into an ideological melting pot rather than establish mechanisms whereby cleavage is openly recognized and accommodated at the political level. It allows all to join in the game providing they keep to the rules; it does not so readily change those rules if people feel unable to co-operate.

39 René Descartes 'Meditation One' in *Meditations on First Philosophy*, ed. Stanley Tweyman, Routledge, 1993, p.46.

40 Richard Rorty *Objectivity, Relativism and Truth*, *op. cit.*, pp.187–188.

41 This is a paraphrase of a Derek Jarman observation on Margaret Thatcher being at the helm of 'Battleship Britain'.

42 Richard Rorty *Contingency, Irony and Solidarity*, *op. cit.*, pp.135–140.

43 PI, §§206–208.

44 Michel Foucault *Foucault Live: Collected Interviews, 1961–1984*, Semiotext(e), 1996, p.8.

45 Michel Foucault *Discipline and Punish*, Peregrine, 1979, p.218.

46 Ibid., p. 138.

47 Richard Rorty *Contingency, Irony and Solidarity*, *op. cit.*, p.65.

48 See Paul Patton 'Foucault's Subject of Power' in *Political Theory Newsletter* Vol.6, No.1, pp.60–71.
49 Paul Patton *Freedom, Power and Subjectivity*, paper given to Humanities Research Centre Conference, 15–17 June 1994.

6 HUMAN RIGHTS AND RULES OF CIVILITY

1 Principles of the good life have a history centred about fundamental disputes at the level of narrative myth, disputes which are central to the being of individual language users. This position is recognized by Stuart Hampshire (*Innocence and Experience*, Penguin, 1989, pp.54–57) who subsequently goes on to talk about the possibility of agreed co-operation based on a common need for stability. It is precisely the motive for this agreement, however, that is in question.
2 Peter Winch 'Certainty and Authority' in A. Phillips Griffiths (ed.) *Wittgenstein: Centenary Essays*, Royal Institute of Philosophy, 1991, p.236.
3 OC §204.
4 Wittgenstein quoted in R. Harris *Language, Saussure and Wittgenstein*, Routledge, 1990, p.68. Also 'Grammar describes the use of the words in the language. So it has somewhat the same relation to the language as the description of a game, the rules of a game, have to the game' (ibid.).
5 As R. Harris illustrates this point is contentious because Wittgenstein was never clear as to how autonomous he envisaged grammar as being. On a weak interpretation grammar could be that which permits language games and forms of life, each differing from each other as to what is to count as truth, regularity and so on. The stronger interpretation is that grammar is the system of rules which determines what is to count as meaning and so has already taken into account external reality. Clearly taking criteria to function as appropriations of objects in the world lends strength to the stronger interpretation (*op. cit.*, pp.80–84).
6 C&V, p.41e.
7 BB, p.17.
8 Such practices or projects need not be conscious or have an overt goal; they can as Loran Lomasky says in *Persons, Rights and the Moral Community* (Oxford University Press, 1987), be either reflective or non-reflective and still maintain their motivational and volitional character (p.44). Similarly, Wittgenstein urged us to resist looking for a reservoir from which actions are always to spring (BB, p.143) or assuming that to use a word, or follow a project, we must necessarily be *accompanied* by a feeling of understanding (BB, pp.155–158). What is reflective and non-reflective, voluntary or involuntary, is in many cases characterized by the circumstances under which action takes place.
9 'The origin and the primitive form of the language game is a reaction; only from this can more complicated forms develop. Language – I want to say – is a refinement, "In the beginning was the deed"' (C&V, p.31e).
10 See Stanley Cavell *Conditions Handsome and Unhandsome*, University of Chicago Press, 1990, pp.90–97.

11 PI, §80, §84, §99.
12 Identity is something Wittgenstein saw as the complex and symbiotic interplay of behaviour and states of mind; it makes no sense to reduce it to anything simple (PI, II, v, pp.179e–180e). This is why he uses the concept of pattern to talk about feelings, something which recurs in the weave of our life, but with potential variations (PI, II, i, p.174e; Z, §§568–569). Feelings are felt, but nowhere specific – we may feel convinced of something, and there are expressions of this certainty (tones, facial movements and so on) – but they are never static, a person's face permits inferences (Z, §514). The type of inference being made varies according to circumstances – though the good Samaritan inferred from observation of the man's evident distress that he needed help, it is not an inference he makes about his own pain behaviour.

> 'Putting the cart before the horse' may be said of an explanation like the following: we tend to someone else because by analogy with our own case we believe that he is experiencing pain too. – Instead of saying: Get to know a new aspect from this special chapter of human behaviour – from this use of language.
>
> (Z, §542)

13 RC, §125. Wittgenstein talks of this as perhaps the flow established between seeming and being in which perspicuous representation is governed by what is imaginable, or what Cavell picks up on in his discussion of normality and naturalness and their providing the 'strength' for criteria to operate (see *Philosophical Passages*, Blackwell, 1995, p.167).
14 RC, §349.
15 RC, §230.
16 See Wittgenstein's discussion of angina as diagnosed sometimes by the rendering of symptoms (inflammation) and at others by defining criteria (the bacillus was discovered). Between these instances there are no hard and fast rules and this does not result in a lack of clarity, because there is no real definition of the concept in any event. 'To suppose that there *must* be would be like supposing that whenever children play with a ball they play a game according to strict rules' (BB, p.25).
17 See David Schalkwyk 'Fiction as "Grammatical" Investigation: A Wittgensteinian Account' in *The Journal of Aesthetics and Art Criticism*, Vol.53, No.3, Summer 1995, pp.287–299, p.289.
18 RC, §124, §69.
19 Wittgenstein observes that Lichtenberg's aphorism that few people have ever seen pure white was intended not an invocation of the ideal as correct, but as an indefinite construction carried to extremes which can teach us about our use of the concept white – that we have, for instance, a kind of geometry of colour ranging from light to dark (ibid., §§35–36).
20 'The queer resemblance between a philosophical investigation (perhaps especially in mathematics) and an aesthetic one, e.g. what is bad about this garment, how it should be, etc.' (C&V, p.25e).
21 C&V, p.24e.
22 PI, §421.
23 Cornelius Castoriadis 'Modern science and philosophical interrogation' in *Cross-roads in the Labyrinth*, Harvester, 1984, p.176.

24 There is great danger in asking for evidential justification for human rights, because it always leaves the proponent open to the possibility of exclusion. The use of factual evidence has been used by many supporters of apartheid in South Africa saying, as they often did, that blacks were not human *because* of their smell, or their colour. The general facts of nature are not evidence in this sense, they are not something we can ostensively define, they are embodied in our grammar to the extent that it is up to us how we treat them. It is in this sense that Wittgenstein tries to get us to change direction completely in the realism/anti-realism debate. Absolutes are possible, but at the ordinary, not metaphysical level.

25 See Murray Bookchin *The Ecology of Freedom*, Black Rose Books (revised edn), 1991, p.5 where he talks of hierarchy as a complex system of control and obedience where elites enjoy varying degrees of command over subjects whom they do not necessarily exploit. Such elites need not be materially wealthy (therefore they are distinct from, though can encompass, Marx's economic classes). Hierarchy is something involving psychological sensibilities towards phenomena at every level of experience. See also M. Foucault in *The Subject and Power* where he talks of power relations being much more than just institutionalized systems (in H. Dreyfus and T. Rabinow *Michel Foucault: Beyond Structuralism and Hermeneutics*, University of Chicago Press, 1983, pp.214–232).

26 J.F. Lyotard in Stephen Shute and Susan Hurley (eds) *Human Rights: The Oxford Amnesty Lectures 1993*, Basic Books, 1993, pp.136–147.

27 C&V p.46e.

28 PI, II, xii.

29 Z, §674.

30 BB, p.157.

31 Richard Rorty *Objectivity, Relativism and Truth*, Cambridge University Press, 1991, p.194.

32 C&V, p.6e.

33 See Michael Oakeshott *On Human Conduct*, Clarendon Press, 1975, pp.9–12.

34 Ibid., pp.120–122.

35 Ibid., p.55.

36 Ibid., p.56.

37 PI, p.206e.

38 PI, p.212e: 'The concept of an aspect is akin to the concept of an image. In other words: the concept "I am seeing it as . . ." is akin to "I am now having *this* image".'

39 PI, p.213e.

40 PI, §611–615.

41 Oakeshott sees action as a performance by virtue of its being an 'illustrative exhibition' of an agent's understanding of themselves and a world of *pragmata* (*On Human Conduct, op. cit.*, pp.34–35).

42 Michael Oakeshott *On Human Conduct, op. cit.*, pp.234–235.

43 Michael Oakeshott 'Rationalism in Politics' in *Rationalism and Politics*, Methuen, 1962, p.3.

44 Ibid., p.5.

45 Ibid., p.28.

46   Ibid., p.11 and Wittgenstein's comments on the imponderable evidence in PI, II, p.228e.
47   Michael Oakeshott *On Human Conduct*, *op. cit.*, p.57 (see also footnote).
48   Michael Oakeshott 'Rational Conduct', in *Rationalism and Politics*, *op. cit.*, p.101.
49   Ibid., p. 105.
50   Michael Oakeshott *On Human Conduct*, *op. cit.*, p.126.
51   Ibid., p.165.
52   *Lex* is an authoritative system to be subscribed to by *cives* when following language games such that they are able to understand themselves and their mutual relations. To do this it must also accommodate or constitute rules for jurisdiction, ascertaining meaning, adjudicating disputes, making revisions and establishing offices and it must expect substantive performances from assignable *cives*. These comprehensive conditions of association, the system of rules followed out of a common acknowledgement of its formal authority and not out of any recognition of its being desirable or good in terms of its providing shelter, being the embodiment of a specific will or being scientifically correct, Oakeshott calls *Respublica*, and as such it is self-authenticating (*On Human Conduct*, *op. cit.*, pp.147–158) – it is understood on its own conditions.
53   See Bhikhu Parekh 'Oakeshott's Theory of Civil Association', in *Ethics*, 106, October 1995, pp.158–186.
54   Michael Oakeshott *On Human Conduct*, *op. cit.*, p.148.
55   Richard Flathman describes these as three types of modes required by Oakeshott to make what is a very abstract and lean idea of civil association have any possibility of being. See his *The Practice of Political Authority*, University of Chicago Press, 1980, p.41.
56   Michael Oakeshott *On Human Conduct*, *op. cit.*, p.167.
57   Though Oakeshott distinguishes between the practice of civility *per se* and that limited aspect of civil living he calls politics: the deliberation of public affairs, which together with the machinery of government, the office of authority and the mode of association go to make up the condition of civil association (see Bikhu Parekh, *op. cit.*, pp.178–180), the political is generally being used, as throughout, in a wide generic sense of institutional relational engagements.
58   Michael Oakeshott *On Human Conduct*, *op. cit.*, p.184.
59   Richard Flathman, *op. cit.*, Chs3–4.
60   Michael Oakeshott *On Human Conduct*, *op. cit.*, p.106.
61   Richard Flathman, *op. cit.*, Ch.5.
62   Ibid., p.106
63   Michael Oakeshott *On Human Conduct*, *op. cit.*, p.146.
64   Michael Oakeshott 'The Voice of Poetry in the Conversation of Mankind' in *Rationalism and Politics*, *op. cit.*, pp.198–199.
65   Michael Oakeshott *On Human Conduct*, *op. cit.*, p.123.
66   Michael Oakeshott quoted in T. Fuller 'The Poetics of Civilized Life' in J.Norman (ed.) *The Achievement of Michael Oakeshott*, 1993, Duckworth, p.73.
67   Michael Oakeshott *On Human Conduct*, *op. cit.*, p.85.
68   Ibid., p.84.
69   Ibid., pp.87–88.

70 Ibid., p.89.
71 Ibid., p.95.
72 Ibid., p.59.
73 Ibid., p.104.
74 Ibid., p.105.
75 PI, II, ix, p.188e.
76 Stanley Cavell, *op. cit.*, pp.24–25.
77 C&V, p.27e.

Index